Ian Rankin's
Black and Blue

CONTINUUM CONTEMPORARIES

Also available in this series:

Forthcoming in this series:

· **IAN RANKIN'S**

Black and Blue

A READER'S GUIDE

GILL PLAIN

CONTINUUM | NEW YORK | LONDON

2002

The Continuum International Publishing Group Inc
370 Lexington Avenue, New York, NY 10017

The Continuum International Publishing Group Ltd
The Tower Building, 11 York Road, London SE1 7NX

www.continuumbooks.com

Printed in the United States of America

Library of Congress Cataloging-in-Publication Data

Plain, Gill.
   Ian Rankin's Black and blue : a reader's guide / Gill Plain.
      p. cm. — (Continuum contemporaries)
   Includes bibliographical references.
   ISBN 0-8264-5244-2 (pbk. : alk. paper)
   1. Rankin, Ian. Black & blue. 2. Detective and mystery stories, Scottish—
History and criticism. 3. Rebus, Inspector (Fictitious character). 4. Edinburgh
(Scotland)—In literature. I. Title. II. Series.

PR6068.A57 B567 2002
823'.914—dc21

                                                            2001047752

Contents

For the crime lovers—Prim and James.

Acknowledgements

Thanks to everyone who helped me get this book together, especially Jill Gamble and the magnificent Lilias Fraser, whose emergency transcription skills made much more possible in much less time.

I greatly benefitted from discussing the book with Helen Boden, Neale Laker and James McKinna—many thanks to them for advice, ideas and expertise. Thanks also to Elspeth Joy at Orion Books, and to David Barker at Continuum for recognising that crime fiction is contemporary too!

Finally, I'm very grateful to Ian Rankin who generously made time to talk to me at length about *Black and Blue*. As requested, Ian, all references to Lacan have been expunged from the text.

1

The Novelist

In February 2001 I spoke to Ian Rankin about *Black and Blue*, the process of writing, and the impact of the novel's success on his career. Unless otherwise stated, all the quotations in this chapter are taken from that interview.

Ian Rankin claims that he did not set out to write crime fiction. He has often told of his surprise, and horror, on finding his first Rebus novel, *Knots and Crosses*, shelved among the detective fiction in his local book shop. Mortified by this categorization, he went as far as to apologize to his lecturers at Edinburgh University, where he was at that point a PhD student. It is a great story—but it does not quite chime with some of his other comments on the merits of the genre. Pressed on the subject, however, he confesses rather to a mercenary appropriation of the form: "I think what I wanted to do was write something that was on the surface a crime novel that was going to sell loads of copies, but which would be accepted by my peers in academia as being serious Scottish fiction". But whatever Rankin's original intentions, crime fiction is what he writes now, and he does it very well. When *The Falls* was published in April 2001, the media reported that he had been offered a £1.3 million contract to keep his detective alive and investigating for another two books. Being a practical man, Rankin accepted.

However, to describe Rankin as a crime writer is to risk subjecting his fiction to an uncomfortable cultural ghettoization. As his own reaction to the categorization of *Knots and Crosses* reveals, the literary world still maintains a division between the highbrow and the popular. An artificial critical boundary separates genre fiction from contemporary writing, and any writer who finds themselves slotted into the genre category will find their books subjected to very different terms of criticism — if, indeed, they receive any critical attention at all. But it is novels such as *Black and Blue* that give the lie to this arbitrary divide, illustrating that genre is not opposed to serious writing, and can actively promote a sustained critical engagement with the pressing ethical and political questions of our time.

The crime novel might be seen, then, as a framework through which the attitudes and beliefs of the contemporary world can be analyzed and explored. Crime writers emerge from diverse traditions and their fiction is shaped by influences beyond what is customarily associated with the genre. Ian Rankin provides a particularly good example of a writer whose crime stories emerge not from a slavish adherence to formula, but rather from its disruption. His novels are, in some sense, hybrid fictions, melding the conventional elements of the police procedural with history, politics and contemporary anxieties. The literary influences that shape his writing are similarly diverse, and in a recent interview in *Scotland on Sunday*, Catherine Deveney quotes "one of [Rankin's] fellow Scottish novelists" on the subject of literary inheritance:

Ian's very keen to tell you he's not a genre writer . . . and actually I don't think he is. I see him as falling into a definite Scottish tradition of adventure stories that goes back to Stevenson and Buchan. But Buchan's adventure stories have no psychological depth and that's where Ian scores. (*Scotland on Sunday*, 25 March 2001, p. 11)

The influence of Scottish writing on Rankin is considerable, and stretches well beyond the most frequently cited debt to Stevenson's *The Strange Case of Dr Jekyll and Mr Hyde* (1886). The fascination with the dark side of cities and individuals alike is also the subject of James Hogg's *The Private Memoirs and Confessions of a Justified Sinner* (1824), a darkly comic fable about evil, self-delusion and the perils of Calvinism, in which the unfortunate central character is persuaded by the devil—or his own desires—that murder and mayhem are justified, as he is one of the elect. The parallels with Rankin's work are evident. He also seeks to expose those who think they are above the law, focusing in particular upon the hypocrisy of the rich, whose money buys them power and the conviction that they are untouchable. Rankin himself, however, takes the connection with Hogg a stage further and stresses the significance of the story for Rebus's relationship with his long-term adversary, the Edinburgh gangster Morris Gerald Cafferty: "Cafferty is a kind of devil who is always standing behind Rebus with this seductive voice, saying 'It feels good to do bad things, why don't you give it a go' ". A final connection to be made with the Scottish literary canon is the link uniting Rankin with Sir Walter Scott. This is not a connection forged through style or theme, but rather a shared concern with history. Scott's historical novels were focused around a fictional hero characterized by his unremarkability, but the margins of the narrative would be filled with 'real' people. As with Rankin's choice of Bible John, Scott would select mythologized figures from Scotland's past—Rob Roy, Bonnie Prince Charlie—and work them into novels that in turn asked questions of the history they were appropriating.

Other literary influences are evident in the texture of Rankin's writing. His fondness for word play means that the names of his characters can seldom be taken at face value, as for example in *Black and Blue*, where the passing mention of an American gangster called Moose Maloney reveals his debt to Raymond Chandler (p. 390). Readers well versed in the genre will recognize the proximity of the name to that of Moose Malloy, the mythical big man hunted by Philip Marlowe throughout *Farewell, My Lovely* (1941). There is a similar nod towards popular culture in the name given to Maloney's associate — Eddie Segal. Rankin's tacit acknowledgement of Chandler emerges from a wider debt to American literature — a subject in which he specialized as an undergraduate. His crime writing, in both style and content, draws on the traditions of the hard-boiled American novel, and Rankin often cites the work of James Ellroy as a significant factor in the later development of his work. A less obvious influence, however, is Anthony Powell's twelve novel sequence *A Dance to the Music of Time*. Powell's novels span three decades, and Rankin found himself seduced by the carefully layered connections that structure the books. Characters come and go across the disparate volumes, achieving varying degrees of importance, the minutiae of one novel becoming the central matter of the next. This was a framework which the serial crime novelist could exploit and develop.

The interconnectivity of Powell, the sharp staccato dialogue of Ellroy, Chandler's isolated hero and the dark side of the human psyche beloved of Stevenson and Hogg: all these influences are adopted, adapted and relocated to contemporary Edinburgh to form *Black and Blue*, a fast-moving crime novel that is also a meditation on evil and human responsibility. *Black and Blue* was the eighth novel to feature Inspector John Rebus of the Lothian and Borders police, and it marked a turning point in Rankin's career. The novel is more ambitious and wide ranging than any of the previous Rebus adventures, and in our discussion Rankin tried to identify exactly what it was that made *Black and Blue* "bigger, better, more complex" than his previous novels:

I think there are a lot of possibilities. One is that I'd just served the apprenticeship. Suddenly I felt more confident that the crime novel could do more than I was doing with it, that I wasn't stretching myself and it was time to do that. Partly, I think, I was just hooked at that time on James Ellroy's novels and I saw this huge landscape that he was using, and his language, and the way he took risks with structure. And also another book I really enjoyed at that time was *Trainspotting*, with the kind of argot that Irvine Welsh actually mainly invented—slang words that I knew didn't exist, because I'd lived in Edinburgh.

From these roots emerged Rankin's own innovations. Uniformed police officers became "woolly suits" and cells became "biscuit tins", devices designed to give the reader a sense of a defamiliarization as they entered a known world that was yet distinctly alien—a literary landscape that they would have to work just a little bit harder than usual to fully understand. Cracking the code of this imagined community, however, would in turn provide the reader with the reward of belonging and an increased engagement with the novel's events and characters. But whatever the reasons for *Black and Blue*'s success, the novel made a huge difference to Rankin's career, a difference that would eventually transform him from a moderately successful producer of critically well-received crime fiction, into a best-selling author with a million-pound book contract.

RANKIN AND THE WRITING OF *BLACK AND BLUE*

Rankin's success as a writer emerged from unlikely beginnings. Born in 1960 in Cardenden, a small mining town in Fife, his more obvious career choices would have been the fast-closing mines, the dwindling ship yards, or the traditional fall-back of the army—a fate he would later visit upon his hero, John Rebus. However, Rankin did well at school and became the first member of his family to go to University, choosing to study English literature at Edinburgh. He enjoyed both the course and the city, and in 1983, after brief exposure to the cold chill of the climate outside academia, Rankin returned to Edinburgh to begin a PhD thesis on Muriel Spark. Again he admits to mercenary motivation. He thought that he wanted to be an academic, and he was told that this was a project that was likely to be funded. Nonetheless, he found himself impressed by Spark's "mindbogglingly bizarre" books, and considers her 1970 novel *The Driver's Seat* to be "absolutely stunning, still one of the best books ever". However, after a year's research he discovered that he was far from alone in studying Spark: "In America there was almost a PhD industry on her". This realisation made him doubt the validity of his own project, and gave substance to a conviction that had slowly been growing within him: "suddenly, about halfway through, I thought what I should really be doing is using this time to write my own books."

The last two years of his thesis funding consequently went towards the completion of three novels: *Summer Rites*, which was never published, *The Flood*, published by Polygon in 1986, and *Knots and Crosses*, which appeared a year later in 1987. This was a time of change for Rankin. Along with his first published novel came marriage to Miranda, and a move to London, where she was working as a civil servant. The couple stayed in Tottenham, with Rankin taking a variety of more or less desirable jobs, until the spring of 1990 when they moved to France. Rankin is comical on the subject of what became an incredibly difficult time:

Miranda says now, "you've got this idea that it was an idyll out there, you just sat writing all day—but you didn't, because the floors were rotten with woodworm and the garden was a mess . . ."

The six years spent in France ended up being far from idyllic. Money remained a perpetual problem throughout their stay, causing Rankin panic attacks, which he attempted to relieve by "driving around the lanes of France at seventy miles an hour screaming at the top of my voice". In spite of—or perhaps, because of—his anxieties, Rankin wrote prolifically during this time. Rebus was re-introduced after a four year absence, appearing in his second investigation, *Hide and Seek* (1991). This was followed in quick succession by *Wolfman* (1992—later reissued as *Tooth and Nail*), *Strip Jack* (1992), *The Black Book* (1993), *Mortal Causes* (1994) and *Let It Bleed* (1995). Each novel was a little longer and more complex than the last, but the financial rewards were still insufficient, and Rankin was forced to adopt a pseudonym, Jack Harvey, under which name he produced a further three thrillers: *Witch Hunt* (1993), *Bleeding Hearts* (1994) and *Blood Hunt* (1995). 'Jack Harvey' was created out of necessity, but he served a useful purpose. In his brief introduction to the reissue of the novels, Rankin recalls that they became a valuable space for experimentation: "they were ways of playing with ideas and structural problems outside the scope of my detective series" (*The Jack Harvey Novels*, p. vii).

The opportunity to experiment through different authorial personae was short-lived. The Jack Harvey novels were not selling, but Rebus, in contrast, was growing in popularity—and as each Rebus novel was taking more and more time to research and write, they became the logical place for Rankin to focus his energies. But even if Jack Harvey had not come to the end of his useful life, it is unlikely that Rankin would have had time to produce any more thrillers. In January 1995 his difficult life in France became infinitely harder when it became clear that his younger son, Kit—then six months old—was seriously disabled. Over the next year, which was also the period of *Black and Blue*'s composition, he and Miranda attempted to deal with the demands of doctors and specialists describing medical conditions in technical French, while driving miles to and from hospitals with their other son, two year old Jack:

All of that went into the writing of *Black and Blue*, I'm sure of it. All of the anger, the frustration, all the questions, and it was like a catharsis for me. In this book I took Rebus down as low as he's ever got . . .

. . . I think that's another thing that made this book different. I was spending a long time writing *Black and Blue* because I was controlling the universe in the novel in a way I couldn't control the world in real life.

Although the initial stimulus was painful, the end product was a significantly different book to any that Rankin had previously produced. For a start, it was twice as long as usual. Rankin recalls that when he started writing he could scarcely imagine producing a book of over 200 pages: "it just seemed such a colossal thing, like running a marathon"—and he, in contrast, was a sprinter—desperately keen to tell his story, and always rushing to get to the end. But *Black and Blue* was different: "I think I knew when I started that it was going to be a long one. There were so many strands to it, so many stories that I was trying to weave in". Both Rankin and his agent were confident that they had something special on their hands, but his publishers were more circumspect, producing a first paperback print run of a moderate 25,000 copies. Rankin had by now returned to Edinburgh, making the publicizing of both the novel and its author considerably easier, but it took the award of the 1997 Crime Writers Association Gold Dagger for fiction to really convince Orion that their home-grown talent had made the leap from middle-list author to international best-seller. This prestigious award is given to the year's best crime novel written in English, and past winners have included Ruth Rendell, Val McDermid, Dick Francis and Colin Dexter. From this point onwards Rankin's work acquired a whole new set of meanings. His backlist had been reissued in a smart uniform jacket, giving an easily recognizable market identity to a "Rankin and Rebus" novel. Readers could now catch up on the past history of their hero and by 1998 Ian Rankin had become the most successful writer in Scotland, setting a new record by occupying 6 out of the top 10 places in the Scottish Book Marketing Group's annual sales survey. And number one on that list was *Black and Blue*.

The books that followed *Black and Blue* continued to enhance Rankin's reputation, and sales continued to grow. While Rankin's early novels received a paperback print run of less than 10,000, *Set In Darkness* (2000) topped 20,000 in hardback sales alone, with paperbacks running well over 100,000 after only a year on the market. By 1998 Rebus had been optioned for television, leading to much speculation in the Scottish press as to who would play the dour detective. In the end the role was taken by John Hannah, and the first novel to be adapted was, appropriately, *Black and Blue*. With the demand for Rankin's novels reaching unprecedented levels, his publishers decided to reissue some of his earlier fiction. In 2000, all three Jack Harvey novels were given the official livery and integrated into the Rankin canon.

Rankin's success has been phenomenal. As well as the Crime Writers' Association Gold Dagger award that he won for *Black and Blue*, Rankin has won the CWA Short Story Dagger twice, been a recipient of a Chandler-Fulbright award and been short-listed for the American equivalent of the Gold Dagger, the Edgar. His books have been translated into 16 languages and sell well across Europe, Canada, and Australia. The American market, however, has been

slower to develop, a problem which Rankin attributes to a reluctance amongst some American readers to accept his ambivalent
attitude towards closure—ironically, one of the factors that has
contributed most to his *critical* success as a writer. From the outset
Rankin's novels have resisted easy answers and tidy endings:

I like loose endings, but crime readers don't always like that, they prefer a
sense of closure. I think this is one of the problems that the crime novel
faces in being accepted as a literary genre. Academics will look at the
closure that you often get in crime novels and say, "this isn't realistic—it's
too pat, too neat, too tidy", and I agree that it's actually debilitating to the
form. But if you try and loosen it up a bit, and don't have any sense of
closure, then you lose a lot of the readers, who have come to the form
because there's a certain comfort in knowing that at the end all their
questions will have been answered, all their worries about the characters
resolved, order will have been re-established in the world and the status
quo will resume.

Rankin's relatively minor success in America is the exception to the
rule, and in Britain, the accolades he has received from the crime
fiction establishment have now been joined by the markers of mainstream literary success. Rankin has been the recipient of two hon-
orary degrees, one from the University of Abertay Dundee and one
from the University of St Andrews, he makes frequent TV appearances as a cultural commentator, and on the July 1st 2001 his
literary credentials were acknowledged by a *South Bank Show* documentary devoted to his work. Rankin is pleased to see evidence of
the gradual erosion of the boundary dividing popular and critical
success. He is delighted that crime fiction is increasingly being
regarded as a serious subject of study, and considers his inclusion
in the South Bank pantheon as "good for the validation of the genre.

It's a wake up call to everybody to say let's not be snobby about this."

AFTER *BLACK AND BLUE:*
THE DEVELOPMENT OF RANKIN AND REBUS

Although Rankin has gone from strength to strength, Rebus's fortunes have fluctuated since the events of *Black and Blue*. In the next novel, *The Hanging Garden* (1998), Rankin continued to pile the pressure onto his hero. The book begins with a hit and run accident that leaves Rebus's daughter, Sammy, in a coma. She regains consciousness at the end of the novel, but three books later in *The Falls* (2001), she is still struggling to recover from her injuries. Rebus, however, spends the entire duration of *The Hanging Garden* tormented by the conviction that he is somehow responsible for Sammy's accident—that this terrible event has occurred simply because of him. Metaphorically castrated by this evident paternal failure, he attempts to compensate by throwing himself obsessively into caring for a witness, Candice, who comes to act as a surrogate for Sammy (p. 38, 48). As with *Black and Blue* several complex plotlines are interwoven. The narratives of Rebus's daughter and witness are accompanied by a particularly brutal version of the Jekyll and Hyde story, in which Rebus must attempt to determine whether respectable Edinburgh citizen Joseph Lintz had a previous life as a Nazi war criminal.

Again Rankin has opened up his favourite territories—the tension between the past and the present, complicity, responsibility and guilt—but he goes even further in his determination to deny his detective the consolations of closure. Rebus can find no explanation for Sammy's accident: it was an arbitrary, chance event. He cannot save Candice from her past any more than he can deal with the demons of his own, and his suspected war criminal is found hanging from a tree long before his guilt or innocence can be determined. And, in a final assault on his detective's already over-developed sense of guilt, Rankin gives Rebus another cross to bear when Jack Morton, his sole support in *Black and Blue*, is gunned down in a botched CID operation.

Jack Morton becomes another of the ghosts that haunt Rebus, and it is ghosts that preoccupy Rankin in *Dead Souls* (1999). This is arguably Rankin's bleakest novel. Rebus becomes increasingly demoralized and disconnected from the present, unable even to find his customary release through work (p. 16). This time the past he must investigate is his own, when a former girlfriend from his teenage years in Fife asks for his help to find her missing son. The novel's other primary concern is with cycles of abuse. The interwoven strands involve pedophilia, institutional child abuse, serial killing and the media, and, as usual, Edinburgh respectability is revealed as a sham. The novel is every bit as well executed as *The Hanging Garden*, but there is something static, or overly familiar, in Rankin's twisting of the knife in his isolated hero. The space inside Rebus's head has become claustrophobic. Rankin won new admirers by tearing his detective apart in *Black and Blue*, but he is aware that "it's not a trick you can pull off every book":

Sometimes readers get a bit cheesed off when Rebus is quite balanced in some of the books, but he couldn't go through the experiences of *Black and Blue* every week—he'd be out of the police, they just wouldn't want him. Since I got back to Edinburgh, I've found out more about how police officers really are, and the books have become more realistic in terms of police work, and I couldn't suddenly make Rebus more of a maverick than would be acceptable to the police.

Rankin's dilemma here is a problem common to writers of serial fiction: whether to stick to a winning formula and keep on providing more of the same, or whether to develop characters and style, seeking new directions within established parameters.

Rankin, wisely, has opted for the second, and in *Set in Darkness* (2000) he takes some of the pressure off Rebus by opening up new perspectives and characters. Relatively speaking, Rebus is indeed "quite balanced" in this book, and in a departure from the trajectory of the previous novels, he works as part of a team trying to uncover the connections between the contemporary murder of a prospective MSP (Member of the Scottish Parliament), the historical discovery of a long hidden corpse, and the seemingly unrelated suicide of Edinburgh's wealthiest tramp. For those who prefer their crime fiction in confrontational mode, however, there is the return of Big Ger Cafferty, out of prison and seeking to reclaim his territory. The town is unlikely to be big enough for the both of them, and while Rebus is pursuing his private battle, a far greater burden of investigation falls on DC Siobhan Clarke. Developing Clarke is a new departure for Rankin, and one that offers considerable scope:

As the books progress Rebus is playing less and less of a role, and other characters, like Siobhan, are playing a bigger role. I wanted to write about Siobhan, I've always thought she was an interesting character. There's a tension in her between playing by the rules, being a kind of mini-Gill Templer and therefore progressing through the ranks, but at the same time she's attracted to Rebus's way of doing things as well. He's almost like the devil at *her* shoulder, saying "you don't have to do it by the book".

And this is exactly what Rankin does in *The Falls* (2001). Siobhan is uncomfortably caught between her inclination to sympathize with outsiders and her own ambitions to fit in. Her instincts draw her towards Rebus's style of policing, but her head reminds her that Templer's by-the-book methodology is the only path likely to lead to success. Sexual politics and competition become newly complex issues as Siobhan attempts to negotiate between the two extremes, but the conflict is not limited to within the lower ranks. Without fully realizing what they are doing, Rebus and Templer compete, like angel and devil, for the soul of their apprentice, Siobhan (p. 143, p. 192, p. 260).

Rankin, then, has established the framework to extend his Edinburgh police novels beyond the natural working life of his original hero John Rebus. The question is whether or not he wants to do this. Over the course of his writing career, Rankin has tried to innovate within the genre and, as his early reluctance to be categorized suggests, there are other literary directions he wishes to explore. If Rankin wants to experiment, however, Rebus and his colleagues might have to depart, as twentieth century literary history suggests that writers have generally been obliged to abandon the police hero if they wish to be taken seriously. This unwritten rule of literary etiquette took shape at the end of the nineteenth century, and Rankin is in no doubt that it is one of Edinburgh's most famous literary sons, Sir Arthur Conan Doyle, who must shoulder the blame for its formulation:

Until Sherlock Holmes came along, it looked like the crime novel was going to be written about serious working police officers. Dickens and *Bleak House*, Wilkie Collins. . . . And then suddenly along comes Sherlock Holmes, this "consulting" detective who never seems to get paid, and the police officer is reduced to a kind of bumbling walk-on part. . . . And it's no accident that this coincides with the police's failure to catch Jack the Ripper. The honeymoon period when the public loved Scotland Yard was over, and we were reduced to having polite intellectuals and amateurs solve the crimes for us. It was terrible—and it was the end of the police officer as hero in English literature for a very long time.

P. D. James, Ruth Rendell and Rankin himself have all contributed to the police officer's gradual return to heroic status, even if the application of the epithet "literary" remains subject to debate. It is certainly becoming increasingly difficult to distinguish general fiction from genre fiction, as more and more "mainstream" writers turn to crime for inspiration. The 1990s saw Jonathan Coe's *What a Carve Up!*, Margaret Atwood's *Alias Grace*, Irvine Welsh's *Filth* and Martin Amis's *Night Train*, to name just a few of the borderline crime novels that have contributed to the problematization of genre status. Rankin does not need to give up writing crime — it looks as if the rest of the literary establishment is coming to join the detective party. But, nonetheless, there are stories that cannot be told this way, and it is possible that Rankin will write them. But only when he's finished the job of pushing his detective, his formula and his city to the absolute limit:

The question I'm always asked now, of course, is do you feel constrained by the crime novel? Is there stuff that you want to do that the crime novel can't do? And I suppose the answer is yes — but, I haven't yet got to the stage of being able to leave the crime book alone, or leave Rebus alone, because I don't think I've said as much as there is to say about him or about Edinburgh, or about Scotland's criminal history. (11)

2

The Novel

Black and Blue is a bleak and complex novel in which criminal investigation is used as a means of exposing the precarious condition of contemporary society. The style is crisp and succinct. Short sentences and bursts of dialogue accumulate without explanation, offering the bare minimum of guidance to the reader who must fill in the blanks and make the connections necessary to comprehend the disturbing and defamiliarized world of the protagonist, Detective Inspector John Rebus of the Lothian and Borders police. Rebus conforms to many of the patterns we have come to associate with the hard-boiled urban detective. He is a hard-drinking obsessive loner, who has difficulty sustaining relationships. He is distrustful of institutional structures and is inclined to privilege his private morality over public law—a tendency which inevitably sets him in conflict with authority.

The novel's structure, however, cannot be so easily summarized, involving as it does four different investigations, all of which overlap, tracing a network of guilt and complicity across the length and breadth of Scotland. The geographical and political scope of Black and Blue is immense. The state of the nation is integral to events in the novel, making the diverse locations active participants in, rather than passive backdrops to, the unfolding narrative. Rankin's Scotland is far from picturesque. As his detective travels the country he encounters the Scotland of big business and vested interests. He sees a nation of internecine rivalries in which traditional landscapes, both urban and rural, are being obliterated by the awe-inspiring but corrosive influence of global corporate capitalism. As Rebus moves between Edinburgh, Glasgow, Aberdeen and Shetland he constantly encounters new challenges — topographical, conceptual, and linguistic — and each location comes to act as a new frontier, complicating the reader's sense of Scotland as a coherent national unit.

The ambitious scope of the novel is matched by the intricacies of its interwoven plots. Rebus variously investigates the death of oil worker Alan Mitchison, found impaled on a spike outside a derelict Edinburgh tenement; the ongoing threat of serial killer Johnny Bible, seemingly the reincarnation of authentic 1960s bogeyman Bible John; the flow of drugs from Glasgow to Aberdeen to the oil platforms of the North Sea; and the re-emergence of a case from his own past — that of murderer Lenny Spaven, who has committed suicide in prison, still protesting his innocence of the crime for which he was convicted by Rebus's mentor, Lawson Geddes. Underpinning these investigations are sub-plots featuring police corruption, corporate greed, the brutality of contemporary society and the collapse of the nuclear family. To offer any further summary of the plot would be self-defeating. *Black and Blue* is a complicated novel, both in terms of the puzzles it presents to detective and reader, and in its blurring of the boundaries between history and fiction. Bible John was real. He terrorized Glasgow in the late 1960s and he was never caught. Johnny Bible is a figment of Rankin's imagination, and between the two cases the novel presents names, places, witnesses and theories that occupy an uncertain territory between fiction, myth and reality. Rankin builds his crime novel on a series of unsolved murders, and in so doing indicates that this will be a book about questions as much as answers.

It is one thing to have four plots in a novel, quite another to build them into an effective narrative whole. Part of the achievement of *Black and Blue*, therefore, is the skill with which Rankin moves between his diverse narrative strands. Using Rebus's somewhat paranoid perspective, Rankin plays with red herrings of conspiracy and connection, letting the detective's fevered imagination make impossible links that keep the various plots alive (p. 253). One of the most effective examples of Rankin's narrative juggling is provided by Chief Inspector Ancram's second interrogation of Rebus regarding his complicity in the Spaven case. As the scene begins, Rankin uses banter to convey the scarcely repressed hostility between the two men—a form of discourse that disguises both male aggression and affection behind a façade of comedy. In this instance, Rebus's wise-cracks are clearly aggressive, designed to challenge Ancram's authority by disturbing his composure. They represent an attempt at self-assertion through verbally undermining the man who actually has all the power. However, as the encounter develops, Rankin uses the scene not simply to progress the Spaven case, but also to develop the Mitchison murder:

"... you were at Inspector Geddes' house, and there was a telephone call?"

"Yes."

"You didn't actually hear the conversation?"

"No." Braid-hair and Mitchison ... Mitch the organiser, protester. Mitch the oil-worker. Killed by Tony El, henchman to Uncle Joe. Eve and Stanley, working Aberdeen, sharing a room ...

"But DI Geddes told you it was to do with Mr Spaven? A Tip-off?"

"Yes." Burke's club, police hang-out, maybe an oil-workers' hang-out too. Hayden Fletcher drinking there. Ludovic Lumsden drinking there. Michelle Strachan meets Johnny Bible there ... (p. 365)

Rebus is grasping at straws, but his segue to Johnny Bible via Uncle Joe and Burke's club has enabled Rankin to resuscitate all four of his plot strands in a single brief exchange.

Technically, then, *Black and Blue* is impressive. It has complexity, suspense and action — but, ultimately, Rankin is less interested in whodunit, or even particularly in why they did it, than in what it means to live in a society in which such crimes are possible. Consequently he constructs not a seamless narrative of cause and effect, but rather a collection of fragments that persistently resist the possibility of coherent reassembly. Straightforward answers are few and far between in the pages of *Black and Blue*, but that does not prevent Rebus from attempting to construct a grand narrative from the ruins. The project is futile, but the detective's attempt to create order out of chaos gives rise to an impressionistic passage of writing that, more than any plot summary, condenses the significance of Rankin's novel:

It seemed part of some larger pattern, accidents forming themselves into a dance of association. Fathers and daughters, fathers and sons, infidelities, the illusions we sometimes call memory. Past errors harped on, or made good by spurious confession. Bodies littered down the years, mostly forgotten except by the perpetrators. History turning sour, or fading away like old photographs. Endings . . . no rhyme or reason to them. They just happened. You died, or disappeared, or were forgotten. You became nothing more than a name on the back of an old photo, and sometimes not even that.

Jethro Tull: "Living in the Past". Rebus had been a slave to that rhythm for far too long. It was the work that did it. As a detective, he lived in people's pasts: crimes committed before he arrived on the scene; witnesses' memories ransacked. He had become a historian, and the role had bled into his personal life. Ghosts, bad dreams, echoes. (p. 461)

Black and Blue is about the power of the past; how we know it, live with it, and come to terms with its secrets and lies. Rankin posits the detective as historian, but even this reinscription is ambiguous. Is the historian's job to preserve or to uncover, and hence rewrite, the past? And to what extent is either activity possible, given the instability of what Rankin calls "the illusions we sometimes call memory"? Certainty is not an option in this novel, and it is significant that in the two historical cases disinterred in the text—those of Lenny Spaven and Bible John—the reader is left devoid of crime fiction's traditional resolution and closure. In the case of Spaven, neither Rebus nor the reader can ultimately be sure of the extent of Lawson Geddes's betrayal. The original reports are obviously disingenuous, while Geddes's confessional letter is, like any piece of first person narration, partial and unreliable. Even Rebus's memory can offer no consolation. He was there, but he cannot be sure that his eyes did not deceive him. He cannot obtain the closure of either certain guilt or innocence (p. 457). In a similar evasion of traditional narrative closure, Bible John slips away at the end of the novel, depriving Rebus of the evidence to support his hunches, and denying the reader the customary climax of criminal confrontation and capture. Answers are replaced by irony, as Una Slocum, unwitting wife to a serial killer, ponders the sexual urges that have caused her husband to desert her for "another woman" (p. 483).

Rebus's interior monologue also emphasizes the novel's concern with issues of betrayal, family ties, inheritance, self-destruction and obsession. He imagines that his public role as custodian of the past has "bled into his personal life" (p. 461) and the image is singularly appropriate, evoking contamination, a loss of definition, and pain. The breaking down of boundaries is central to *Black and Blue*. Past and present, public and private, innocence and guilt, certainty and doubt—all are destabilized as Rebus's investigations expose not their difference but their proximity. The detective yearns for a world in which black and white are clearly demarcated, but is faced instead by the almost unbearable knowledge of his own complicity. And, just as Rebus has been contaminated by the guilty secrets and violent actions of his everyday investigations, so the novel suggests, with its emphasis on inter-connectivity, that we all are implicated in the "criminal" state of contemporary society. As Rebus walks the streets of Glasgow and Edinburgh, he sees two cities in which wealth and prosperity sit side by side with embattled poverty and despair. This urban deprivation does not simply coexist with comfortable complacency—the two are fundamentally linked. The hypocrisy that underpins respectable society is a constant theme within Rankin's fiction, and the desire to expose this duality installs him within a tradition of Scottish writing exemplified by Stevenson and Hogg, whose influence was discussed in Chapter 1. This concern with duality, however, also does much to explain his choice of crime fiction as a medium through which to shape his contemporary fictions.

GENRE AND CONTEMPORARY FICTION

[C]rime fiction deals with contemporary issues in a way that the literary novel is refusing to. If you look at the Booker and Whitbread shortlists, there's an awful lot of looking back, and not much about what's becoming of us in this new Internet age, this corporate age, this leisure industry age. Crime novels and thrillers are the ones dealing with that. (Ian Rankin, interviewed in *The Bookseller*, 9 February 2001)

Rankin believes that, at its best, crime fiction represents the cutting edge of contemporary writing, engaging with issues that more mainstream or "highbrow" fictions refuse to approach, and resisting the nostalgia and insularity often cited as characteristic of contemporary British fiction. But what does it actually mean to write crime fiction? To what extent is it appropriate to call *Black and Blue* a crime or detective novel? And is an understanding of genre useful for interpreting Rankin's approach to the contemporary novel?

Crime fiction, or the detective novel, is customarily seen as having two main categories: the cozy, classical model, sometimes referred to as "golden age" fiction and exemplified by such writers as Agatha Christie, Dorothy L. Sayers and Margery Allingham; and the hard-boiled American version, typically associated with the fiction of Dashiell Hammett and Raymond Chandler. The classical model has its roots in the rational certainties of the seemingly omniscient detective, Sherlock Holmes — but its "golden age" is associated with the interwar period (1920–1939), when the formula evolved into what some critics have suggested was a parodic response to the carnage of World War I. The reckless heroics, casual bloodshed and confident outlook of Imperial Britain were replaced in Agatha Christie's fiction with a vision of an inward-looking, domestic England, while the assertive masculinity of Sherlock Holmes was rendered redundant by the "little grey cells" of the effeminate outsider, Hercule Poirot (Stephen Knight, *Form and Ideology in Crime Fiction* [1980]; Alison Light, *Forever England* [1991]). Although its inception can be seen as historically specific, the classical form continues to thrive, and endless variations can be found of its basic premise. A murder is committed in an enclosed environment — a village, country house, boat, plane, train or whatever, and a detective outsider is brought in to identify the killer. In its traditional form the village was, paradoxically, both a site of prelapsarian ideality and a hotbed of scarcely repressed and violent passions. The village represented a desirable status quo, a community worthy of protection that deserved to be rescued from its cancerous criminality by the surgical skills of the analytical detective. Yet, at the same time, the formula required that the community must be a guilty one. Everyone must be a suspect, harboring secrets and at the very least, guilty intent. In identifying the actual criminal, however, the detective acts as a father confessor. A criminal scapegoat is identified and the community is conveniently absolved of its guilt.

Guilt is less easily evaded in the other main category of crime fiction. "Hard-boiled" crime fiction emerged from the pulp magazines of the American 1920s and, in the words of Raymond Chandler, it "gave murder back to the kind of people who commit it for reasons, not just to provide a corpse" ("The Simple Art of Murder", p. 195). The location shifts from the predominantly rural to the predominantly urban, and the albeit imperfect community of classical crime fiction is replaced by a fragmented landscape of alienation, corruption and decay. Unsurprisingly, the change of location requires a change of detective, and the hard-boiled formula meets the challenges of the city through the iconic figure of the tough guy detective, famously described by Chandler as:

a complete man and a common man and yet an unusual man. He must be, to use a rather weathered phrase, a man of honour, by instinct, by inevitability, without thought of it, and certainly without saying it. He must be the best man in his world and a good enough man for any world. . . .

. . . He is a common man or he could not go among common people . . . He is a lonely man and his pride is that you will treat him as a proud man or be very sorry you ever saw him. He talks as the man of his age talks, that is, with rude wit, a lively sense of the grotesque, a disgust for sham, and a contempt for pettiness. ("The Simple Art of Murder", p. 198)

Chandler's description paints a posthumous coat of whitewash over many of the earlier manifestations of the tough-guy hero, but it nonetheless captures the spirit of rugged individualism that the private eye inherited from the American West.

The genre's change of detective is naturally accompanied by a change in the process of detection. The hard-boiled detective is involved rather than detached, implicated both physically and emotionally in the corrupt landscape under investigation. Unlike the classical detective, whose mode of detection transcends the body, the tough guy's investigation is rooted in the body. His weakness for the *femme fatale* leads him to follow heart rather than head, and his pursuit of the criminals is more often based on gut feeling than rational deduction. Chandler's Philip Marlowe is typical in his tendency to detect through confrontation: he puts his body on the line, inviting attack as a means of proving the guilt of those he accuses. The beating of the detective is a staple of the hard-boiled formula. It symbolizes the toughness of the hero—encoded more in his capacity to endure than in his ability to fight back—and it illustrates the strength of his convictions, proving that he is not a man who can be persuaded from the path of righteousness. The scars on his body thus come to mark him out as the custodian of truths that society would rather not hear. Here and elsewhere I have been using "he" to describe the hard-boiled detective, because this form of crime writing is focused around constructions of masculinity, and although the female private eye has now become a popular figure, in the early days of the genre, she was conspicuous by her absence.

In today's literary marketplace this is the mode of crime writing that has triumphed, both in terms of sales and contemporary relevance. The classical formula continues, but it is not the sort of fiction to which Rankin is referring when he argues for the importance of the genre. The hard-boiled model has been adopted and adapted to enormous effect by such writers as James Ellroy, Lawrence Block and Sarah Paretsky, and Rankin cites the contemporary American crime novel as a key influence on his writing. *Black and Blue* notably opens with a quotation from Ellroy—albeit adapted to acknowledge Rankin's formative debt to the Rolling Stones—and in many respects it is Ellroy whose work provides the most useful point of reference for an understanding of Rankin's project. In his introduction to *Criminal Proceedings*, a collection of essays examining the diversity and significance of the contemporary crime novel, Peter Messent offers a succinct account of Ellroy's fiction that illustrates the shared concerns of the two writers:

The disorientating narrative tactics he uses (as compared to the majority of detective fictions) challenge standard generic expectations. For the confusing landscape of his novels—the moves between different locations, events, and narrative perspectives, the rapid-fire movement of his elliptic prose, and the sheer number of his characters—works at a textual level to suggest the problematic nature of any authoritative negotiation of the complex and labyrinthine city world he depicts. And, in the thoroughgoing nature of his destabilising of the agency and identity of his detective subjects, he radically challenges the sense of individual autonomy, objectivity and authority on which the detective genre has tended traditionally to rely. (p. 17)

With the notable exception of the multiple narrative perspectives, Messent could as well be describing *Black and Blue*. But Rankin's success is not simply a case of transatlantic appropriation, and the Rebus novels are shaped by a multiplicity of other influences that work to fundamentally reinscribe the already problematic figure of the hard-boiled hero.

In the first instance, as Rankin has observed, hard-boiled detection cannot be straightforwardly transplanted from America to Scotland:

I think it was Raymond Chandler who said that if the action was beginning to get a bit slow, you just had to have someone come through the door with a gun. Well, that's fine in LA but it's not so good in Peeblesshire, or St Andrews, and so you've got to think of other ways of dealing with crime in that context. (Interview with Ian Rankin, *Scotlands*, 1998 p. 108)

The appearance of realism is integral to the fantasy of the detective novel, and plausibility demands that the cerebral dimension of the classical tradition retains at least a partial hold on the British crime narrative. The second factor mitigating against the straightforward adoption of the hard-boiled generic template is the private investigator himself. The PI is a figure with certain built-in limitations. Peter Messent, for example, argues that "the marginal position and limited perspective of the PI hero or heroine makes for an ineffectual, and even irrelevant, figure as far as the representation of criminal activity and its containment goes" (1997: 2), and for this reason Rankin, like many others, has turned to the police in order to create a viable structure of investigation.

The police procedural is a sub-genre of crime fiction that emerged in the late 1950s and has come to dominate the market both in terms of fictional sales and television adaptations. Probably the most famous writer of procedurals is Ed McBain, and his long running series of 87th Precinct novels has been instrumental in establishing the dramatic concept of the "police family". This vision of a group of diverse individuals working together for the common good has come to dominate fictional representations of the police, but the model has been avoided by Rankin, who has chosen instead to make his policeman an increasingly isolated outsider. Rebus is not one of a team — but, nonetheless, the fact that he is a policeman has obvious advantages, as Rankin explains:

I chose a policeman because they have access to all areas. He is the perfect figure because he can go to the Lord Provost's private residence and ask questions, he can go to a junkie-filled tenement in Niddrie and ask questions; no doors are going to be closed to him or, if they are closed, they won't be closed for very long. (Interview with Ian Rankin, *Scotlands*, 1998, p. 106)

The state-sponsored authority of the police undoubtedly enables a vast range of investigative possibilities, and British society in general remains willing to maintain the necessary fiction of policing as a protective rather than a repressive force.

Yet, although superseded and, in some sense, impractical, the PI is far from dead, and on closer inspection, many of the Rebus novels, including *Black and Blue*, owe a conspicuous debt to the model of the individual loner detective. Just like Philip Marlowe, Rebus must plough a lone furrow in search of a truth nobody wants him to uncover. Frequently, the object of Rebus's investigative zeal is institutional corruption, and he is isolated from his police colleagues by his refusal of the pragmatic compromise. He is similarly isolated in private, as most of his personal relationships have been destroyed by his obsessive commitment to work. In neither his home nor his work life can he be described as a "family" man. According to his private moral agenda, the rights of the victim almost always outweigh the convenience of the system, or indeed, the rights of those who survive the victim. This capacity to pursue a "higher" truth at whatever cost is made clear in *Let It Bleed*, the novel immediately preceding *Black and Blue*, when Rebus's boss, Chief Superintendent "Farmer" Watson, accuses him of a selfish disregard for others:

". . . these obsessions of yours end up damaging everyone around you, friend, foe and civilians alike.

. . . As long as your own personal morality is satisfied, that's all that counts. Sod everybody else, isn't that right?" (*Let It Bleed*, p. 269)

The similarities between contemporary policeman and archetypal private eye are also evident in the number of beatings that Rebus takes over the course of *Black and Blue*. But, as with his predecessors, any attempt to "warn him off" is counterproductive: the violence to which he is subjected simply acts as physical evidence in support of his theories (p. 234). And the toughness of the hero is not confined to the body. Hard-boiled detectives are also characterized by the ability to talk tough, a skill which Rebus demonstrates in his encounter with the oil tycoon "Major" Weir. Their brief mid-air meeting emphasizes both Rebus's independence and his lack of respect for authority. He refuses to be cowed by the patriarch's power, and deploys the tough-guy's archetypal weapon, the wise-crack, in an attempt to bring the arrogant Weir down to size:

"Can I ask you something, Major? Why did you name your oilfield after an oatcake?"
   Weir's face reddened with sudden rage. "It's short for Bannockburn!"
   Rebus nodded. "Did we win that one?" (p. 209)

In view of the evidence, it is not surprising that Rebus spends much of *Black and Blue* on the run from both police and criminals alike. He acts, in effect, as a private eye within the police force, enabling Rankin to have his cake and eat it too—preserving the myth of the heroic individual in the midst of the more "realistic" police narrative of co-operative investigation.

   To a certain extent, the myth of the heroic individual is a necessary one, which perhaps accounts for its continued prevalence in both film and contemporary fiction. The actual nature of the heroism has changed over the years to admit flaws and complexity—heroism has become more *difficult*—but the concept of an individual agent has become, if anything, a more vital fantasy than ever in an increasingly global age. Policemen, like most of us in the computer age, represent a small cog in a very large machine. Serial killers are not found by charismatic individuals, but through the painstaking accumulation of detail, through data entry and cross-referencing, through actions that never see a chain of cause and effect, let alone an end product. Hence the continued appeal of the maverick, the man or woman who resists the system, and the need, within the new sub-genre of serial killer fiction, for the fantasy of the inspired individual — be they psychological profiler, pathologist, or the rogue cop who will not play by the rules and insists on following gut instinct over procedural rationality. Asked by Ludovic Lumsden whether he found anything in Shetland, Rebus's response is typical: "Just a bad feeling. A little hobby of mine, I collect them" (p. 232).

Rankin's version of the heroic myth is a sophisticated one that manages to problematize the category at the same time as putting it to effective dramatic use. Rebus is the classic maverick — in the words of Jack Morton, an "irregular regular" (p. 372) — a selfish, self-obsessed control freak who cannot trust others to do the job, but who is nonetheless made sympathetic by his evident emotional investment in the case. The privileging of an emotional response to crime solving is a key dimension of the Rebus novels, and in *Black and Blue* the detective's pain is an integral part of the narrative. Rebus suffers in this novel, but this is not the result of the physical pain from his beatings — indeed, such assaults seem actually to provoke a masochistic regeneration of the detective. Rather his pain emerges from an inability to distance himself from the suffering of others. Although he tries to resist it, he is haunted by the victims he encounters, and he takes their pain onto himself, tearing himself apart through his excessive identification and feelings of responsibility:

People died and you couldn't bring them back. Some of them died violently, cruelly young, without knowing why they'd been chosen. Rebus felt surrounded by loss. All the ghosts . . . yelling at him . . . begging him . . . shrieking . . . (p. 381).

Rebus's heroic masochism represents a significant feature of one of the novel's central concerns — the pressures surrounding contemporary masculinity. However, before I move on to consider the themes of the novel in greater detail, it should be noted that there is one other generic form which is key to the structure of Rankin's novel. Although self-evidently a crime novel about a serial killer, *Black and Blue* ultimately builds its drama on the foundations of the western.

Although the western and the hard-boiled detective narrative share roots in the American West, there are aspects of the former that seem particularly resonant in relation to *Black and Blue*. The Western offers many potential narrative strategies, but arguably its most memorable legacy to popular culture is the stand-off. Two (or more) men confront each other and struggle for domination through a literal or figurative duel. These skirmishes between sheriffs and gun fighters, between the law and the outlaw (or even, in the case of Rebus and Ancram, the law and the law), are the dramatic linchpins of *Black and Blue*. Rebus, the lone gunfighter, rides in to confront the outlaws and clean up the town. In Glasgow he tackles the wily old gangster Joe Toal, running the city from his council house, aptly nicknamed "the Ponderosa" (p. 99) — after the long-running 1950s TV serial *Bonanza*. In Aberdeen his adversary is corrupt sheriff Ludovic "Ludo" Lumsden, and his mission is to establish who really runs the town (p. 231). In between the detective's encounters with the villains, the novel is peppered with the classical stand-offs of competitive masculinity. Rebus versus Ancram, versus Cafferty, versus Breen, versus Weir, versus Grogan — whether the violence is verbal or physical, the point is to assert authority, or to restore a sense of control, through out-punching, out-talking or out-staring those males who threaten him. A significant absence in the list of authority figures against whom Rebus asserts himself is, of course, DCI Gill Templer, but her status is fundamentally different because of her gender—a point to which I will return later.

By permeating Rebus's urban investigation with the raw brutality of the western, Rankin reiterates another of his central concerns—the precarious state of Scottish respectability, which he repeatedly stresses is a construct founded on hypocrisy and deceit. Sophistication is peeled away to reveal the violence beneath apparently civilized society, and the values of both are subject to scrutiny. As the novel progresses and Rebus travels further north, the concept of the frontier develops a further resonance. Evoking a significant tradition in American literature, the frontier becomes a place of escape, a cleansing site of "natural" danger, where a man can reconstitute himself away from the corrupt and corrupting influence of "civilization"—usually associated with women and domesticity, but in the case of *Black and Blue*, located in a form of smooth, corporate masculinity.

Black and Blue, then, might aptly be described as a frontier narrative. It is fundamentally concerned with borders and boundaries—the points at which law and social structures unravel to be replaced not by chaos, but by violent and threatening mirror images of themselves. The novel does not present crime as an isolated incident or a force that erupts spasmodically and which can easily be contained. Rather it is an organized structure—a competing system—and Rankin pits this criminal system against the embattled forces of the law. The besieged status of Craigmillar police station is emblematic of the imperiled state of the city itself (p. 6), and once again Rankin draws upon both the hard-boiled and western traditions as he dispatches his detective to "Fort Apache, the Bronx" (p. 22).

THE CITY, THE FRONTIER AND THE LAW:
BOUNDARIES IN *BLACK AND BLUE*

It was Edinburgh's hardest posting; a stint of duty lasted two years max, no one could function longer than that. Craigmillar was about as tough an area as you could find in Scotland's capital city, and the station fully merited its nickname — Fort Apache, the Bronx. [. . .] Being up an alley meant a mob could cut it off from civilisation with ease, and the place had been under siege numerous times. [. . .]

Rebus knew why he was there. He'd upset some people, people who mattered. They hadn't been able to deal him a death blow, so had instead consigned him to purgatory. (p. 6)

The tensions of the frontier are not eradicated by the "civilisation" of the city. Rather, the outlaw goes underground and is reformulated as a type of monstrous in-law. The successful urban criminal creates a fiefdom, an alternative system of government within the city boundary, and polices this territory as thoroughly as any official regulatory force. This is the power structure which Rebus tries to manipulate when he visits Big Ger Cafferty in Barlinnie (pp. 86–7), and it is the structure he must confront when he leaves his own patch, or territory, and travels to Glasgow. Arriving at the Glasgow housing scheme that is home to Uncle Joe Toal, Rebus is confronted by a landscape of "fortified shops" (p. 89), where kids with "eyes as keen as sentries" circle the police car like "a cherokee party with scalps on their minds" (p. 94). This is "a city within a city", and the usual rules do not apply. As a nervous policeman observes to Rebus: "This is the frontier, sir. The frontier has a way of keeping its own law and order" (p. 90).

But Rankin's western imagery isn't simply a convenient shorthand for lawlessness. Rather it represents the tip of an iceberg, signaling the novel's concern with social exclusion, deprivation, and hopelessness. Indeed, so bleak is the urban environment that the description of Niddrie, site of Alan Mitchison's murder, moves over the frontier into a landscape of war:

The place was if anything bleaker by day: blocked-in windows, glass like shrapnel on the tarmac, kids playing in the sunshine with no real enthusiasm, eyes and mouths narrowing as his car cruised past. (p. 103)

Childhood is impossible in such a location, and the kids can only manage a semblance of play. They live in a closed community, under siege in a different way to Fort Apache, but nonetheless imperiled, and their narrowing eyes and mouths represent a pulling-up of the communicative drawbridge. Strangers — outsiders — will not be admitted, particularly if they are representatives of a police force which cannot actively serve or protect them.

By populating his alienated urban landscape as much with children as with adults, Rankin reiterates his concern with the victims of contemporary society. "Mean" streets might be obligatory within hard-boiled fiction, but Rankin is more concerned with depicting the "collateral damage" emerging from urban crisis than in imagining a romanticized gangland. This lack of romanticism extends also to the supposed protectors of the innocent. Rankin is not simply indicting the criminal world in his portrayal of Niddrie and the other scenes of poverty and deprivation that recur throughout the novel. These places are also the victims of "criminal" neglect by central government. They are the forgotten underside of Edinburgh's respectability and Glasgow's new-found prosperity. For Rankin, crime is located not only in individual acts of evil and wrong-doing, but also within the institutional structures of society itself. Consequently, he does not seek to create a "scapegoat" in the manner of traditional crime narratives, but instead depicts a disturbing symbiosis in which crime is both a product of and a producer of wider social structures. Urban life has the potential to generate crime, and crime in turn has the power and organization to structure and reshape urban society.

In the same way that "respectable" society can be seen to be complicit in much of the criminal activity in *Black and Blue*, so the city is more than just a setting within which individual dramas are enacted. Interviewed in 1998, Rankin observed that "Edinburgh is a character" in his Rebus novels, and the detective's relationship with this character is crucial. Rankin's Edinburgh is a dubious, Janus-faced character — its elegant appearance masking a violent underside not immediately apparent to the visitor. Much the same could be said of Aberdeen, where Rebus feels disorientated by his lack of intimacy with his surroundings (p. 165, p. 187). The policeman must be intimate with the city in order to know it and police it, and it is not surprising then that when Edinburgh is personified it takes the guise of an upper-class whore. "Fur coat and nae knickers, that's Edinburgh" (p. 93) observes Uncle Joe Toal, offering a Glaswegian's clichéd perspective on the city. Nonetheless, his image is appropriate and it also serves to remind the reader of two of Rankin's favorite sources of inspiration, the outwardly respectable robber Deacon Brodie, and Stevenson's *Dr Jekyll and Mr Hyde*.

The untrustworthy body of the city is one that needs constant surveillance. In *The Naked City: Urban Crime Fiction in the USA* Ralph Willett argues that:

The best known figure in the study of modern urban experience is the *flâneur* . . . he provides a surrogate for the watchful (male) detective of popular fiction, one who listens, searches and above all, like the private 'eye', sees and deciphers the signifiers of that labyrinth of populated spaces and buildings which forms the modern metropolis — strange and menacing but also intoxicating. (pp. 2–3)

The flâneur is an idle spectator who lives vicariously upon the lives around him — someone who watches, but is not involved — and is superficially an ideal model for the detective. But, while Rebus might be said to have the vision to decipher the "modern metropolis", he cannot be seen to have the detachment of the archetypal flâneur. Rebus is rather an agent who must engage with and, therefore, risk contamination by, the seething mass of the city.

The problem of contamination is a serious one. The personified city is also an embodied city, and like any body it is subject to disease. It is also a mass of bodies, and the infection of crime spreads quickly within crowded and confined spaces. Rankin's vision of urban life emerges as fundamentally dystopian as Rebus, the would-be agent, realizes the extent to which he too is subject to forces beyond his control:

Niddrie, Craigmillar, Wester Hailes, Muirhouse, Pilton, Granton . . . They all seemed to him like some horrible experiment in social engineering: scientists in white coats sticking families down in this maze or that, seeing what would happen, how strong they'd have to become to cope, whether or not they'd find the exit . . . He lived in an area of Edinburgh where six figures bought you a three-bedroomed flat. It amused him that he could sell up and be suddenly rich . . . except, of course, that he'd have nowhere to live, and couldn't afford to move anywhere nicer in the city. He realised he was just about as trapped as anyone in Niddrie or Craigmillar, nicer model of trap, that was all. (p. 106)

Being part of the city, having a sense of place, enables Rebus to understand, if not to condone, the crime he sees. It also, however, exacerbates his sense of powerlessness. Generally speaking, the detective cannot resolve the underlying malaise that gives rise to a criminal society, he or she can only deal with the isolated eruptions of violence, the "obvious" manifestations of criminality. It is a case of policing rather than solving crime. However, in *Black and Blue* a substantial dimension of the detective's "heroism" emerges from his stubborn efforts to move beyond this impasse. Throughout the novel Rebus attempts to fight both the individual criminal and the system that creates criminality. His sympathy for the human lab-rats at the bottom of the city's food chain situates him on a border between the law and its transgression, and puts him at odds with the third "power block" of contemporary society—big business. Like the criminal counter-cultures of the cities, big business establishes its own fiefdoms—it is a law unto itself. Lumsden hints at this power when he describes Aberdeen as "strictly corporate" (p. 182), and Rebus finds that the "nice" roads of Shetland are "[p]aid for with oil money" (p. 416). The power of the multi-nationals is even implicit in the restructuring of the police force: one Assistant Chief Constable has been replaced by a "Director of Corporate Services" (p. 106). Whatever the title actually means, the implication is that the police are there to serve the interests of the business community. Rebus, however, resists the influence of these financial masters. He is not satisfied with policing the small fry, he actually believes he can net the big fish of both the criminal and the corporate worlds, and it is this naiveté that gives Rebus his romantic dimension as a champion of the underdog, and semi-heroic protector of the weak.

Significantly, though, Rebus's willingness to overlook "small" transgressions in order to achieve a higher goal renders him an unstable custodian of the law. I suggested earlier that Rebus operates as a PI within the police force, but in *Black and Blue* he is positioned still further beyond the bounds of legitimacy as two sets of investigators attempt to reinscribe him as actively criminal. By Chapter 11 Rebus is being described as "on the run" (p. 155) from Ancram's internal investigation into the Spaven case, but this early suspicion of criminality is as nothing to the fate which will befall him on his return from Aberdeen, when his obsession with Bible John leads to him being treated as a suspect in the Johnny Bible investigation. That the detective could find himself in quite such an awkward position emphasizes the legal and moral ambiguity of Rebus's actions, and renders him a very borderline detective indeed. Scarcely in control of himself or his investigations, the character of Rebus pushes the template of the flawed hero to the limit, and in so doing provokes a series of questions regarding the shifting gender roles of contemporary society.

GENDER TROUBLE 1: THE PROBLEM WITH WOMEN

"Do you know how many women make chief inspector in the Scottish force?"

"I know we're talking the fingers of a blind carpenter's hand." (p. 113)

Rebus is a detective "on the verge" and while some of his problems emerge from the traditional crime narrative's conflict between heroic individualism and systemic constraint, others are rooted in the more fundamental constraints of gender.

Interviewed in 1998, Rankin claimed that he couldn't write about women (p. 117), but the remark was perhaps a touch disingenuous. On the evidence of *Black and Blue*, and indeed most of his oeuvre up until *Set In Darkness* (2000), it is probably fairer to say that he simply does not write about women. This has begun to change in the more recent novels as Rankin has developed the character of Siobhan Clarke, using her perspective as well as Rebus's, giving her a degree of investigative authority and allowing her to occupy the somewhat uncomfortable position of protégé. However, in *Black and Blue* women tend to occupy familiar roles and are sketched competently, but in less detail than some of their male counterparts. Even Rebus's old friend and ex-lover, Chief Inspector Gill Templer, is kept at a distance from the reader. We see her only in relation to Rebus and are given no access to the range of her private feelings. Instead we see only the vulnerability that emerges from her precarious position as a promoted woman within the patriarchal, misogynistic structure of the police force.

There are a number of possible reasons for this limited perspective. In the first instance, Rebus is the primary focalizer within the novel. Although the narrative is written in the third person, it is his perspective that dominates throughout, and we are witness to very little that has not been mediated through his eyes. The reader is forced to see the world as Rebus sees it, and he cannot be accepted as a wholly reliable narrator. Although we are occasionally treated to a glimpse of Jack Morton's thoughts, the only other significant focalizer is the serial killer Bible John, and in making this choice, Rankin highlights the implicit connection between the two men. He also establishes Rebus as loner—a man out of step with the times—who cannot adequately communicate with the men around him, let alone the women. In establishing this communicative crisis, *Black and Blue* conforms to the templates of both the western and the hard-boiled crime novel. Men and women inhabit separate spheres—even if they do the same job—and in generic terms Gill Templer's function is simple: she is there to be rescued.

The limited roles available to women in genre narrative have been the subject of considerable critical commentary, but in short they are offered a choice between the deadly, sexually voracious *femme fatale*, the asexual (and hence unthreatening) plucky girl assistant, or the damsel in distress, who might double as the victim. All three categories are covered by *Black and Blue*. The appropriately named temptress Eve Cudden brings down the Toal dynasty, while still finding time to treat the detective to a well-earned good time (there is also an interesting resonance in Eve's surname: the

Scots dictionary defines a "cudeigh" as a gift or bribe, "a night's entertainment due from a tenant to his superior"). Rebus later describes her as a "hard nut to crack" (p. 441), applying a cliché of masculinity to a woman whose weapon is her evidently female body. Traditionally, however, this is the danger encoded in the *femme fatale*—she breaks free from the customary association of woman with passivity and emotion, displaying instead a "masculine" appetite for pleasure, power, and independence. She cannot be controlled as she is too wayward, and her fate, therefore, is death. Rankin thankfully revises this outcome, and it is significant that Rebus admires, rather than recoils from Eve's manipulative behavior. However, he cannot resist the temptation of animal imagery, and Eve is compared to a cat, "same morals, same instinct" (p. 386), a comment that reminds us of women's essential otherness—the distance between them and the supposedly male qualities of rationality and humanity.

The second category, that of plucky girl assistant, is filled by Siobhan Clarke. She does not have a large role in the novel, but her brief appearances are significant. The novel features an ongoing motif of inheritance, examining the relations between fathers and their offspring. In the earlier Rebus novels, Brian Holmes had been established as Rebus's spiritual "son", the detective who would take over his maverick mantle and continue the good fight against the forces of evil and corporate policing. However, as I will discuss later, the line of patriarchal inheritance is breaking down in *Black and Blue*, and the clues are laid to suggest that Rebus's legacy must be entrusted to a daughter rather than a son. It is significant that of all the characters in the novel, only Siobhan shares Rebus's instinctive understanding of the familial dynamic at work in the serial killer case: "It might sound crazy, but maybe Bible John's out there looking for his offspring" (p. 395). In her willingness to think the unthinkable, Siobhan proves herself a worthy protégé and inheritor.

However, in this novel, most of her work falls into the assistant category. She works on the inside to find answers for the outsider detective (p. 462), which in gender terms might be seen as an inversion of the norm. However, the book's stress on the changing nature of policing suggests that the force has been domesticated — it has become a sphere of constraint and limitation from which the truly masculine detective must flee. Siobhan, as a woman, can safely negotiate this space, and she is given clues by the paternal Rebus as a reward for her good behavior (p. 396, p. 462).

The final category, that of damsel in distress, is reserved for Gill Templer. Although technically his superior, she needs Rebus to help her survive in the big bad boy's world of the police. The relationship between the two of them becomes that of teacher and pupil, but it is also significantly gendered. Gill needs Rebus because she recognizes that she will have to take risks to make her mark upon the hierarchy. But in the shifting landscape of gender prescriptions, risk is a man's business: women are sensible, and therefore limited. To be sensible is, at least implicitly, to be cowardly — and Rebus's reckless actions throughout the novel tacitly undermine his eventual praise for Gill's careful handling of the drugs case (p. 452). Rebus is operating in a world of changing values and gender roles — shifting sands that are difficult for both men and women alike. Yet, in his relationship with Gill Templer what emerges is not so much co-operation as an ironic inversion of the concept of the "power behind the throne". Where once women's only hope of influence in a patriarchal society was to whisper in the ears of their husbands, brothers and lovers, now the old-fashioned hard man finds himself on the outside looking in. Rebus may not aspire to the acquisition of indirect power through his relationship with Gill, but the events of the novel repeatedly suggest that he could have done her job *if he'd wanted to*. But what self-respecting hard man would seek promotion within the self-serving, appearance conscious and increasingly feminised space of the modern police force? Gill's promotion is rendered ambiguous by its context and rewritten as a consolatory fiction. Irrespective of her ability, her rise is read not as a straightforward reflection of her value as a police officer, but rather as a sign of the times. And, as the novel's concern with history makes clear, Rebus is a man out of step with the times (p. 25, p. 52). There is, however, consolation to be found for the wounded masculinity of the redundant male. Having given Gill the "gift" of Stanley Toal (p. 393), Rebus muses that "[i]t could be the making of her" (p. 426). For men unable to cope with modernity, one route to compensation lies in the colonization of the familial role, seeing themselves as a parent dispensing wisdom — giving away as a gift that power which has in fact already been taken from them. Women may think they are in control, but Daddy knows best.

However, to suggest a paucity of female representation, or to claim that Rebus has problems adapting to the modern world, is not to imply that *Black and Blue* lacks insight into gender issues, or that Rankin is unsympathetic to women. Far from it, in fact. In his sketches of Gill Templer, Siobhan Clarke and Kayleigh Burgess, Rankin succinctly posits the difficulties facing women who attempt to compete in a man's world. Rebus is learning to face up to a similar problem. He too is becoming one of the disenfranchised, and his experiences make him surprisingly aware of the uneven playing field of gender, as the casual encounter with a Glasgow journalist reveals:

She smiled: lip gloss, eye-shadow, tired face trying for enthusiasm. "Jennifer Drysdale." Rebus knew why she was tired: it was hard work acting like "one of the boys". Mairie Henderson had told him about it — the pattern was changing only slowly; a lot of surface gloss about equality sloshed over the same old wallpaper. (p. 97)

But ultimately, it is not through the representation of women that Rankin chooses to ask questions about gender. Rather, *Black and Blue* is a book about men and the relationships that bind or divide them. Over the course of the novel Rankin exposes masculinity as a complex and contradictory construct—a fraught set of historically contingent imperatives which shape, and all too frequently overwhelm, the individual male.

GENDER TROUBLE 2: BIG MEN IN CRISIS

Behold the Scottish male, at his happiest when in denial
                                        (*The Hanging Garden*, p. 223)

The prescriptions of patriarchal masculinity, or the "law of the father", are powerful and difficult to evade. The crippling pressures they can exert on the male subject are made evident from the outset of *Black and Blue*. When Rebus hears the news of Lawson Geddes's death, he struggles to access the emotion he feels over the loss of the man who was, in figurative terms, his father:

He sat in his chair by the window, thinking of Lawson Geddes. Typical Scot, he couldn't cry about it. Crying was for football defeats, animal bravery stories, "Flower of Scotland" after closing time. He cried about stupid things, but tonight his eyes remained stubbornly dry. (p. 45)

Interestingly, Rebus blames his emotional constipation on his nationality, not his masculinity; but in actuality it is difficult to divide the two. To have a national identity, in both historical and contemporary terms, is to be a man. Women's relationship to nationality has traditionally been portable. It transforms on marriage into the national identity of her immutable male other. Rebus's vision of Scottishness is consequently a vision of Scottish masculinity, of the sentimental camaraderie located in the predominantly male arenas of the football stadium or the pub. The gender landscape of these locations might be changing, but as Rebus's encounter with the Glasgow journalist suggests, it will take a lot of gloss before the original wallpaper is obliterated. Nonetheless, what makes men cry is understood to be group emotions, not individual pain. To expose one's pain is instantly to become less than appropriately masculine, it is to be weak, vulnerable, in a word—"feminine". Male mourning is about the silent withholding of emotion. The defenses that go into building the strong façade of masculinity must not be let down. The body must present a firm boundary, its integrity must be absolute—and tears would represent a betrayal of the traditional masculine ideal.

Yet, over the course of *Black and Blue*, Rebus will break down in tears not once but twice, and on neither occasion can his pain be legitimized by the loss of a football match. What does this say about his masculinity and about Rankin's development of the hard-boiled detective? What is the status of the hard man in contemporary society and the modern police *service*? Rankin's novel offers a clear indication of the impossibility of continuing to see masculinity as a single monolithic construct. Like femininity before it, it needs to be broken down to reveal the internal contradictions and tensions that go into its construction. It needs to be revealed as something rooted not in nature, but in an evolving social context. Rebus belongs to a category of masculinity that is fast becoming defunct. He is something of a dinosaur, constructed in the era when hard men had a value in society, when the predominant mode of Scottish masculinity was the working-class ideal of the independent artisan. This figure was a skilled worker and a hard worker, a man of few words and no frills. What you saw was what you got. You might not like the wallpaper, but at least it wasn't covered in gloss, and you could guarantee there was nothing beneath it. He dates, in effect, from a depth model of masculinity. But the world, and masculinity within it, is changing. As industrial capitalism is usurped by the service industry, and consumers become more significant than producers, so a new masculinity is emerging that places a far higher value on surface appearance. This is the framework within which Rebus interprets the smooth performance of Ancram and his team of well-polished Glasgow policemen. He recognizes that the world is changing — but he does not like what he sees, and his instinctive dislike of Ancram emerges from his conviction that anyone with a coat of gloss must have something to hide (p. 102).

The critic Michael Kimmel has written extensively on the historical forms of masculinity, and his work offers a useful template for an examination of Rebus. Throughout this chapter I have been describing Rebus as a hybrid, an amalgamation of policeman and private eye. This duality also has resonances in terms of masculinity and power. CI Ancram acts as a personification of much larger political structures — he symbolizes new, and in Rebus's eyes, corrupt forces of government and policing that seek to feminize the traditional detective by depriving him of agency. These forces are motivated by expediency and pragmatism, seeing the law in shades of grey, and seeking to debar the heroic male detective from his noble, individualistic quest for justice, truth, and certainty. In Michael Kimmel's terms these are "marketplace men", and they represent a new mode of masculinity that has been evolving alongside capitalism over the course of the nineteenth and twentieth centuries. Rebus, in comparison, belongs to the eighteenth century, a period in which the predominant models of masculinity were the "genteel patriarch" and the "heroic artisan". According to Kimmel, these two figures were symbiotically linked. Although their class status differed, they worked through co-operation and respect rather than competition, which is the mode *par excellence* of marketplace man.

Thus Rebus, as an heroic artisan, must fight off the threats to his autonomy (and to the interests of justice and truth) represented by marketplace man. That he is in this position, however, indicates that the mode of masculinity he represents — the Scottish hard man — is in crisis. It is no longer a dominant, but rather a nostalgic mode of being. *Black and Blue* examines this crisis on both a national and an individual level. As Rebus heads north, Rankin recounts the mythical narrative of the "oil rush". The story tells of how men migrated north in search of a new frontier — a place where they could prove themselves, and make their fortunes, through the traditional male role of confronting the elements:

For working-class males based south of Aberdeen, it seemed like the word made flesh, not just a man's world but a hardman's world, where respect was demanded and bought with money. It took only weeks for the switch: fit men came back shaking their heads, muttering about slavery, twelve-hour shifts, and the nightmare North Sea. (p. 164)

There is no place for the "big man" anymore, not even on the platforms of the North Sea, where the roustabout of legend has been replaced by skinny bespectacled computer operators (p. 248). The situation thus suggests that the hard man must evolve or die. Jack Morton, disturbingly for Rebus, has evolved, but throughout *Black and Blue* Rebus is himself in crisis, torn apart by the contradictory demands he faces. To evolve, in his understanding, is to compromise, and the reader is encouraged to sympathize with this point of view, as the values exhibited by marketplace man are repeatedly revealed to border on the inhuman. Yet Rebus also recognizes that the work-obsessed ethos he inhabits is ultimately a self-destructive one, and he mourns the family he has lost through his refusal to abandon his excessive commitment to the job. But to abandon his work is more easily said than done. It is primarily work that gives identity to the male subject, and Rebus's sense of self is dependent upon his continued performance in the role of policeman (p. 372). But while he struggles with the demons of self-delineation, in political terms he is becoming increasingly marginalized — a factor that in part accounts for his ability to understand the difficulties of women attempting to be "one of the boys".

Rebus is not the only character to feel the contradictory pressures of being a heroic artisan in a market-driven service economy. As I suggested earlier, Brian Holmes, the theoretical inheritor of Rebus's detective craft, breaks down under the conflicting demands of public and private spheres. In Holmes's case the impossibility of reconciling the mutually exclusive roles of working man and family man results in an explosion of violence — the only mode of articulation available to men trained to repress rather than express their emotions. To survive in the modern world the policeman, as much as the criminal, must become a manifestation of Jekyll and Hyde:

Brian Holmes: friend. Difficult to equate with the person who had roughed up Mental Minto. Schizophrenia, the policeman's ally: a dual personality came in handy . . . (p. 138)

A masochistic paternal lineage is in evidence stretching from Geddes through Rebus to Holmes (p. 318). Holmes acknowledges this inheritance when he claims he has had a "good teacher" in Rebus, but, as his scraped knuckles show (p. 319), what he has actually learned from his mentor is the art of turning his violent frustrations inwards. He has learnt to beat himself up rather than others. But whether Rebus can be seen as a good father or bad, ultimately he is powerless to stop his "son" leaving the police force (p. 493), and in a destabilizing shift similar to the transformation of Jack Morton, the hero's legacy must be handed to a daughter rather than a son.

Holmes's departure adds a further note of bleakness to the overall tone of the novel. Rebus is certain that abandoning the role that defines him, his police career, will ultimately destroy rather than save Holmes—but we only have Rebus's perspective on this situation. He judges Holmes from the knowledge that it would be unthinkable for him to make the same decision. Brian's resignation arrives at the very end of the novel, undermining the positive news that precedes it, and contributing to what Rankin has described as his ongoing project of "getting rid of all Rebus's baggage" (1998: 116). Yet although the following two novels, *The Hanging Garden* (1998) and *Dead Souls* (1999), will continue a remorseless process of isolating the guilt-ridden detective, *Black and Blue* offers a perhaps illusory respite in the form of male friendship. When Ancram sets Jack Morton to "mind" Rebus, he inadvertently does the tortured detective a favor, providing him with a source of kindness and support singularly lacking in his life. When Jack moves into the flat a restorative pattern of homosocial nurturance evolves, in which a feminized Jack tends the physical and emotional wounds of the persistently masculine Rebus.

To invoke a homosocial relationship is to speak of the permitted relationships between men that cement the bonds of patriarchal society. Homosocial relationships are the chemistry of buddy movies, TV dramas and the western. From *Lethal Weapon* to *Starsky and Hutch* to the Lone Ranger and Tonto, heroes have found solace in the company of their partners. Homosociality comprises a set of unwritten, but nonetheless rigorously policed, rules allowing a carefully calibrated intimacy between men. Too close a proximity and you risk the transgression of homosexuality. Not close enough and you remain, like Rebus, the perennial outsider, devoid of comfort and the understanding that surpasses the love of women.

DI Jack Morton is an interesting character. One time traditional hard man, he has adapted to survive in a changing environment (p. 287, p. 292). In the face of self-destruction he has chosen to save himself—a project about which Rebus cannot help but feel ambivalent. Morton has given up smoking, joined Alcoholics Anonymous, and bought himself a brand new suit—all of which leaves him looking almost indistinguishable from the dreaded marketplace man. His actions also signify a refusal of risk—he no longer wishes to put his life on the line in order to prove his masculinity—and this refusal might be seen to feminize him in the terms of Rebus's understanding of what makes a man (p. 294). Indeed, the role that Jack comes to take in Rebus's life is a curious combination of mother and lover. Like the good woman of legend, Morton helps the hero in his hour of need, cooking the dinner and redecorating the primitive log cabin in which the lonely hero had been sheltering. All that's missing are the gingham curtains. The hero both welcomes and resents this intrusion of the feminine: he does not want to give up his old bachelor ways, but cannot help noticing the benefits accruing from the love of a good woman. After all, it is through Morton's tender care that Rebus enjoys his first decent night's sleep in years (p. 330).

The homosocial bond can also be read in terms of a brotherly dynamic, in which deep affection can only be expressed through the double-edged discourse of banter. I used the term "banter" earlier in this chapter to describe one of Rebus's encounters with Chick Ancram—a relationship in which there is little evidence of brotherly love. In that instance, banter represented a skirmish in one of the central conflicts of the novel. John Rebus and Chick Ancram are the dominant males of the text, and each of their encounters is shaped around a verbal struggle for supremacy. However, banter is more commonly used as a coded expression not of enmity, but of affection. Given that constructs of masculinity prohibit the open expression of love between men, banter has evolved as a means of expressing the ties that bind within a patriarchal society. In *What A Man's Gotta Do*, Anthony Easthope offers a succinct definition of the concept:

The content of banter has a double function. Outwardly banter is aggressive, a form in which the masculine ego asserts itself. Inwardly, however, banter depends upon a close, intimate and personal understanding of the person who is the butt of the attack. It thus works as a way of affirming the bond of love between men while appearing to deny it. (pp. 87–8)

Banter can thus encode both competition and consolation. It asserts masculinity, while articulating possibilities of caring otherwise denied to men, and much of the dialogue between Rebus and Morton takes the form of banter. These exchanges represent the tip of the iceberg, for there is always more going on underneath — questions that cannot be asked and feelings that cannot be expressed (pp. 287–8, p. 445).

The displaced nature of this mode of articulation returns me to the problem of male emotions: the tension between repression and expression. Brian Holmes, unable to speak about the loss of his wife, lashes out at a suspect, imprinting his pain upon the body of Mental Minto. Rebus, too, is riven with such internal tensions, and is equally unable to articulate his frustrations. Not surprisingly, his attempt to hold it all in is as unsuccessful as Holmes's — and the ensuing eruption is positively volcanic. In the fight with Jack Morton all Rebus's firm masculine boundaries collapse into an explosion of emotion:

Teeth bared, Rebus swung again, even more wildly, giving his friend plenty of time to dodge and launch a punch of his own. Rebus almost defended himself, but thought better of it. Instead, he waited for the impact. Jack hit him low, the sort of blow that could wind a man without doing damage. Rebus doubled over, fell to hands and knees, and spewed on to the ground, spitting out mostly liquid. He went on trying to cough everything out, even when there was nothing left to expel. And then he started crying. Crying for himself and for Lawson Geddes, and maybe even for Lenny Spaven. And most of all for Elsie Rhind and her sisters, all the victims he couldn't help and would never be able to help. (p. 325)

Rebus's hard masculine exterior has metamorphosed into a leaky, feminized body. He vomits, he coughs and, above all, he cries — and his tears encode his powerlessness in the face of grief and guilt.

But does this bodily explosion signal a change in Rebus, or in the model of masculinity that he inhabits? It is difficult to say. Perhaps the fight represents a cathartic rebirthing — after all, Rebus certainly feels better for it — but to achieve this release he had first to lash out at his friend. Perhaps then it is fear as much as catharsis that is being expressed in the fight: Rebus is in flight from the pressures and responsibilities of adult masculinity. Significantly Jack Morton observes that he hasn't had a fight like this one since he was a teenager (p. 325), and this regression highlights the particular paradoxes that surround the "achievement" of manhood. Adult masculinity is founded on a paradox in that it encodes both resistance to and control of civilization. In a patriarchal society, the son must accept the authority of the father in order to ensure the line of succession. Consequently, as Freud hypothesized, the child must put aside his violent and unlawful desires (to challenge the father and possess the mother) and find another object/woman through which to mark his independent status as a man in a man's world. This is the form of masculinity coded as rational, contained, firmly bounded and unemotional. But however refined the surface may become, masculinity cannot wholly evade the impulses of childhood aggression. Although brought under control, these transgressive desires do not go away. They form instead a differently valorized dimension of masculine identity—a dimension that is legitimised through violence and competition. This bodily masculinity represents a staging post, something that will be laid aside as the male progresses up the hierarchy, but in Rebus's inarticulate violence a refusal of this progression can be detected. Although every inch the big man, he remains in an ambivalent relation to adulthood.

Yet there is a third possible explanation for the particular character of the fight on the Meadows. Close attention to the encounter links Rebus's behavior to the masochistic dimension of his personality. As Jack launches his punch, Rebus actively decides not to defend himself and waits for the impact to arrive. Rebus wants to be punished. He has a desire to be beaten stemming both from his guilt over the Spaven case and, more fundamentally, from his own "original sin". Rebus is on the verge of self-destruction because at the same time that he needs to preserve a set of essentially "masculine" attributes, he also feels guilty for being a man.

After his first encounter with the dangerous Eve, Rebus retreats and contemplates the conditioning that has established a gulf between him and the opposite sex. From his teenage years he remembers the threat of the father as much as the desire for the girl, from his army days he remembers only sexism and stereotypes, and from his working life he recalls his seduction by the "all-consuming" power of the job. Once again it seems that the past controls the present, and there can be no escape from the man that history has made him:

The problem lay somewhere inside him, and it hadn't been eased by things like the Johnny Bible case, by women abused and then killed. Rape was all about power; killing, too, in its way. And wasn't power the ultimate male fantasy? And didn't he sometimes dream of it, too?

He'd seen the post-mortem photos of Angie Riddell, and the first thought that had come to him, the thought he'd had to push past, was: *good body*. It bothered him, because in that instant she'd been just another object. (p. 190)

Rebus's obsession with the serial killers Johnny Bible and Bible John thus emerges less from a sense of righteous indignation, than from a knowledge of his own contamination. That he briefly saw the likeable Angie Riddell not as a person but as an object indicates the narrow line that divides Bible John's pathology from "normal" male desire. It is not that big a step from thinking of women as bodies or catches, to the serial killer's description of murder as a "cull" (p. 195). Throughout the book Bible John refers to his victims as "it" (p. 118), and this dehumanization acts as an ironic counterpoint to Rebus's excessive, and compensatory, identification with the victims he could not save. By investing their memory with symbolic weight, and carrying it with him wherever he goes, Rebus attempts to atone for his sins through the miracle of resurrection.

GUILT, SELF-DESTRUCTION, PAIN AND THE TRUTH

Jack forced a smile, lifted his glass. "John, tell me though, why do you drink?"

"It kills my dreams."

"It'll kill *you* in the end, too."

"Something's got to."

"Know what someone said to me? They said you were the world's longest surviving suicide victim." (p. 310)

The Rebus of *Black and Blue* is driven by self-destructive impulses. I suggested earlier that these tensions emerge from a crisis of masculinity, but in the final section of this chapter I want to briefly explore some of the other factors that contribute to the detective's pain. This project, however, might be compared to the opening of Pandora's Box, creating a plethora of new issues and debates. The ensuing questions will not necessarily be resolved but should instead be seen as subjects for further discussion beyond the boundaries of this book.

In the early Rebus novels Rankin depicted his hero as a troubled man seeking answers in religion. Rebus would try a different church every week, looking for some elusive consolation and, for a while, he found some outlet for his disputational Calvinism in conversations with a Catholic priest, Father Conor Leary (*Mortal Causes*, pp. 15–21). By *Black and Blue*, however, he has largely abandoned formal religion, and is left with only the painful residue of Scotland's dominant creeds: Catholic guilt and the Protestant work ethic. Rebus cannot rest from feeling guilty.

Rebus's guilt is an important factor in understanding his self-destructive impulses, but these impulses can also be seen to emerge from his highly developed masochistic sensibility. Masochism, the condition of taking pleasure from pain, can be both physical and psychological. The hard-boiled detective has always been characterized by an element of masochism—a certain amount of pain has to be endured to achieve the gratification of toughness—but Rebus's strand of masochism is more closely aligned to psychological models. In her comprehensive study of transgressive masculinities, *Male Subjectivity at the Margins* (1992), Kaja Silverman describes the condition of "Christian masochism", a particular version of self-punishment that can be symbolised through the figure of Christ—the man who took the sins of the world onto himself, who died that others might be saved:

. . . Christ nailed to the cross, head wreathed in thorns and blood dripping from his impaled sides. What is being beaten here is not so much the body as the "flesh," and beyond that sin itself, and the whole fallen world.

This last target pits the Christian masochist against the society in which he or she lives, makes of that figure a rebel, or even a revolutionary of sorts. In this particular subspecies of moral masochism there would thus seem to be a . . . desire to remake the world in another image altogether, to forge a different cultural order. (pp. 197–8)

The connections with Rebus are clear. The emotionally and physically battered detective fights for truth, justice, and a system that serves the victims rather than the manipulators. Rebus is beaten for the sins of the fallen world, a world that includes the police force that will not believe in him.

Kaja Silverman goes on to suggest that Christian masochism has "radically emasculating implications" in its emphasis on ridding oneself of all earthly possessions. Rebus's empty flat can certainly be read as evidence of this divestiture, and his lack of possessions distances him from the race of male acquisition, but it nonetheless seems to me that masochism can equally function as a means of reaffirming masculinity. I suggested above that Rebus sees himself as tainted, implicated in the crimes that he must also fight, and in taking this burden of guilt upon himself, he ironically empowers himself through punishing himself. The threatened status of the hard man is, at least temporarily, reasserted through the capacity for endurance. Rebus creates pain for himself by taking responsibility for all the suffering he witnesses — from the victims of Bible John (p. 381) to his supposed nemesis, Lenny Spaven (p. 325). He alone can bear the burden of caring about these lost lives, he alone can feel their pain (p. 294). But at the same time as he beats himself with the sins of the whole fallen world, he also nurtures and sustains the fantasy that he can redeem these sins. Such a belief empowers the detective, raising him above those whose plodding, by-the-book methods will never avenge the victims of crime. Rebus the detective-savior can put the world to rights, because he alone is the custodian of the truth.

Rebus's relationship to truth is as fraught as his negotiation of guilt, not least because truth itself is a complex concept within the novel. Rebus is a far from conventionally truthful person. Throughout the novel he tells lies for his own convenience, lies that save him from having to explain his gut feelings and high-risk plans. But the novel also focuses on the lies of his past (p. 306–7) — the lies he told out of loyalty to Lawson Geddes, lies which he believed were in the service of a higher truth. Rebus distinguishes between an everyday or "venial" truth, and a far greater concept which might be termed a "mortal" truth: a matter of life and death.

Mortal truths are an integral part of Rebus's obsessive behavior. He cannot accept approximations, he has to know exactly what has happened and why — a characteristic that is perhaps most brutally exposed in *Dead Souls* when Rebus insists that a suicide's widow give him the insight into her dead husband that will finally confirm his theories (p. 385). The same intrusive truth-seeking is present in *Black and Blue*:

I'm a peeper, he thought, a voyeur. All cops are. But he knew he was more than that: he liked to get involved in the lives around him. He had a need to *know* that went beyond voyeurism. It was a drug. (p. 329)

Rebus's obsessive need to know is reiterated as he gets closer to the answers that tantalize him (p. 347), but as the book repeatedly makes clear, his addiction is ultimately destructive. *Black and Blue* suggests not that the truth is out there, but rather that it is an impossible concept. The truth can never be known. It is significant that after the murder of Martin Davidson, Rebus feels that "Bible

John had cheated him out of Johnny Bible" (p. 477). What Bible John has actually done is deprive him of answers — the closure that might have been achieved had we known *why* Johnny Bible did it. Although obviously inspired by earlier killers, this fact is not enough, it does not even begin to explain why a man would wish to worship and copy gratuitous acts of evil. The reader never meets Johnny Bible, and he, like Bible John, remains an ultimately unexplained (and hence more frightening) phenomenon.

There is, however, another dimension to Rebus's "problem" with the truth. In *Black and Blue*, and indeed in many of the other novels, he becomes a Cassandra figure. He speaks the truth, but is destined never to be believed — a fate that could drive anyone to the verge of madness. Like a modern-day soothsayer he reads the signs of deceit around him, detecting the duplicity of Lumsden, the corruption in Glasgow and the truth about Bible John. His premonitions are not always wholly accurate (it is not Ancram who is "bent", but one of his team), but he believes both in their veracity and in the necessity of speaking them. Rebus is unable to be silent, he will not accept political expediency, even at the cost of his own security (p. 102). The compulsion to speak *his* truth is thus a largely self-destructive one, making his job, the pursuit of detection, not so much a vocation as an exercise in martyrdom. Not for nothing is he described as "the world's longest surviving suicide victim" (p. 310):

Time had seasoned his cynicism. He wasn't a terrier now: he was a fighting dog with locking jaws. You just knew that no matter how bloody he got, how much pain there was behind the eyes, the grip was there to the death . . . (p. 373)

At the beginning of *Black and Blue*, Rebus's posting to Craigmillar police station is described as consignment to purgatory (p. 6). At the end of the novel he tells Jack Morton that he is happy where he is, a location he describes as "[s]omewhere north of hell" (p. 493). Rebus's superiors really need not have bothered dispatching him to Fort Apache the Bronx. He is quite capable of experiencing eternal torment in the comfort of his own home. As I have suggested in my descriptions of his masochism, Rebus finds a paradoxical comfort in pain—it reassures him that he is making an impact. Pain tells him that he is not himself a ghost (p. 329), and that he can continue, like Sisyphus, to roll his rock of truth up the mountain of venality that is the modern marketplace world.

Rankin's detective is not a figure who can restore the world to order or make everything "all right". Rather he is an isolated obsessive, struggling to hold himself together in the face of new demands and new threats, taking refuge in the past to avoid the failings of the present, and clinging onto the fantasy that the little guy, the individual investigator, can make a difference. But, for the reader the fantasy is a slender one. We see the world through the bleak perspective of Rebus's eyes (p. 311). We witness the "bland monstrosity" (p. 340) of evil through the parallel detective story of Bible John's hunt for Johnny Bible. And, ultimately, we are left with a knowledge not of the clear-cut distance between good and evil, but rather of the frightening proximity between hunter and killer, the law and its outlaws.

3

The Novel's Reception

Black and Blue could perhaps be described as a slow starter. Although most early reviews were positive, its critical reputation has grown over time, acquiring kudos both from the award of the Gold Dagger and from the success of Rankin's later novels. Certainly the novel is now regarded as an important book that opened up new horizons for its author and for the Scottish crime novel. Nick Hasted, surveying Rankin's career in *The Guardian* described *Black and Blue* as "a book with epic reach" (21 April 2001), and its combination of narrative excitement, moral crises and political acuity have made it a frequent choice in Scottish schools for independent studies. The book's popular success contributed to a growing demand that more serious critical attention be paid to the crime novel, a point made emphatically by Alan Massie in his review of Rankin's next novel: "Ian Rankin confirmed his reputation with *The Hanging Garden*, a novel which suggested that the categorisation of fiction into straight and crime novels is obsolete" (*The Scotsman*, 5 December, 1998).

The initial reviews of *Black and Blue*, however, were mixed, voicing reservations that in some cases said as much about the critic's prejudices as they did about Rankin's novel. *The Irish Times* is a case in point. Reviewer Michael Painter was not happy to find a crime novelist getting ideas above his station, and in a brief review he describes the book as a "rambling odyssey". Painter does not seem to have found the book worthy of close attention, which perhaps accounts for his misguided claim that Rebus was complicit in framing the original Bible John—but it is his conclusion that most clearly states his position on the distinction between "literature" and the popular:

At almost four hundred pages, the book is much too long, but with its adipose tissue slathered off it would have been excellent of its type. Rankin is much too good a crime writer to become bogged down in issues, so let us hope that in his next case Rebus returns as lean, mean and laconic as he used to be. (*The Irish Times (Dublin)*, 22 March 1997)

Painter firmly believes that it is not the business of crime fiction to engage with the "real world". Marilyn Stasio in *The New York Times Review of Books* believes otherwise, and tells a very different story in a short but largely positive review. Stasio acknowledges the tradition within which Rankin is writing, describing his novels as "so gritty you have to pick the shards out of your teeth when you finish one", and her somewhat flippant tone suggests that she was not wholly convinced by the connections that drive Rebus's investigation. Nonetheless, her conclusion roundly refutes the notion that crime fiction has nothing to do with "issues":

Rankin has a point to make about the corrosive effects of human wickedness that, if left unchecked, seeps into the bloodstream and poisons the national body—a point well made in his blunt and bruising style. (*The New York Times Review of Books*, 14 December 1997)

Some of the mixed responses that greeted the novel emerged from the fact that *Black and Blue* was a substantially *different* Rebus novel. Marcel Berlins, writing in *The Times*, was emphatically in favor of the change: "This is the book Ian Rankin has threatened for some time. Others in the Inspector Rebus series have been uniformly first rate: *Black and Blue* outreaches them in excellence"—but Peter Whitebrook in *Scotland on Sunday* sounded a more cautious note. Like Marilyn Stasio he was impressed by the moral dimension of the novel and argued that in the construction of his detective Rankin had "transformed a commonplace article from the genre cupboard into something entirely his own". However, he also had reservations: "*Black and Blue* feels less like an achievement in itself than a novel which may come to be seen in retrospect as the bridge between one phase of work and another" (26 January 1997). Whitebrook suggests that the writing is actually *too* economical for the length of the novel. He feels that Rankin's "stylistic palette is still that best suited to the preceding shorter and more compact novels". Nonetheless, Whitebrook finds plenty to praise, and his description of the novel as transitional is prescient in terms of the later development of Rankin's career. He also has no reservations about the role of crime fiction in contemporary literature, seeing Rankin as "a romantic storyteller in the tradition of Robert Louis Stevenson". Whitebrook argues that although "Rankin uses much of the equipment of the detective genre, his ambitions are clearly those of the literary novelist":

His books are tales well told of crime solved, yet order is never wholly restored from chaos and there is always the disturbingly pervasive sense that the devil, once inside us, leaves an indelible impression. (*Scotland on Sunday*, 26 January 1997)

Whitebrook's praise acknowledges the experimental dimension of Rankin's writing and his capacity to exploit the tension between resolution and uncertainty. For other critics, however, it was Rankin's wider agenda that made the most substantial impact.

Writing in *The Literary Review* in January 1997, Philip Oakes argued that:

Rankin captures, like no one else, that strangeness that is Scotland at the end of the twentieth century. He has always written superb crime fiction — and this novel maintains the standard. But what he's also pinning down is instant history. Whether or not it's how we choose to remember it, this is how it's really happening.

Oakes here acknowledges that, to his mind, Rankin had succeeded in his stated aim of producing a book about Scotland — a "state of the nation" novel. Ten months later, after the award of the Gold Dagger, Boyd Tonkin in *The Independent* consolidated this point. Tonkin expanded on the importance of crime fiction as a literary form, arguing that "good crime writing can reach those social parts that more genteel operators dare not investigate":

Rankin certainly merits his Gold Dagger for the sheer cunning of his intrigue and the morose, but oddly moving realism of his hero's dysfunctional existence. One further twist lifts *Black & Blue* above the ruck: a vivid grasp of the oil boom and its transforming impact on so much Scottish — and, indirectly, British — life. Rankin depicts the Wild North with a fascinated relish that has precious few rivals in the "literary" novel. How many Selfs or McEwans could take us into the raucous frontier-town dives of Aberdeen, through the vast Shetland terminal at Sullom Voe, or onto the platforms planted in the icy waves? Yet North Sea oil is one of the great hidden themes of modern British culture . . . It needs its chroniclers in fiction as well as fact. (*The Independent*, 12 December 1997)

High praise for Rankin, and a reminder of the then still predominantly metropolitan focus of the contemporary British novel.

Yet in marked contrast to this positive response, cultural critic Liam McIlvanney found Rankin's Scottish novel lacking in bite.

McIlvanney's review in *The Times Literary Supplement* was particularly vexed by the writer's "superficial and unsatisfactory" treatment
of Bible John: "It is striking that this novel, which features a real-
life killer, seems far less engaged with contemporary Scotland, far
more of a hermetic literary puzzle, than many of Rankin's earlier
books" (28 February 1997). Marcel Berlins disagrees, calling the
"introduction of a perhaps still-at-large killer" a "brilliant device".
But McIlvanney's complaint is not that Bible John was a bad idea,
but rather than Rankin had failed to capitalize on his "daring gam-
bit" — a failure that reduces the character's appearances to the "level
of a gimmick". McIlvanney's praise is reserved instead for Rankin's
earlier fiction, in particular *Mortal Causes* and *Let It Bleed*, which
"engaged intelligently with central aspects of Scottish society".
McIlvanney's final complaint is Rankin's style, which he claims is
"less assured than usual", composed of "chatty, almost slapdash
prose", and his review is probably one of the harshest the novel
received (although I am discounting here a review from *The Bir-
mingham Post* which opened with the claim that "Ian Rankin's
novels are all set firmly in Glasgow"). Given the belief of so many
critics and, indeed, Rankin himself, that this was the novel in which
he was really trying to push himself to develop both his writing and
the crime fiction form, it is curious to find McIlvanney concluding
that the novel lacks "brio and ambition".

It is perhaps testimony to the scope of *Black and Blue* that it
prompted criticism on so many fronts. For William Painter it ex-
ceeded the remit of the crime novel, becoming entangled in "issues". For Boyd Tonkin and Marcel Berlins it effected a
harmonious alliance between place and pace, taking the reader into
territory beyond genre. And for Liam McIlvanney it simply wasn't
Scottish enough. But however extensive McIlvanney's criticisms, in
one respect his review was a triumph, located as it was not in a
crime fiction ghetto, but in the general fiction section of a "highbrow" literary paper.

4

Rebus on Screen

Not surprisingly, given the seemingly insatiable appetite of the British public for television crime dramas, *Black and Blue* has been awarded the accolade of TV treatment. In April 2000 Scottish Television and Clerkenwell Films screened a single two hour drama staring Scottish actor John Hannah as Rebus. The idea of a TV Rebus had been in the air for some time, and in 1998 *The Scotsman* (30 January 1998, 14 February 1998) speculated about who might play the leading role. Rankin was quoted as expressing a preference for Bill Paterson, who had already played Rebus on the audiotape of *Black and Blue*, but it was not until Hannah's production company picked up the option that the drama actually went into production. Rankin felt Hannah was "too young, too clean" for the part (*The Bookseller*, 9 February 2001) and initially expressed no desire to see the adaptation. The *Sunday Telegraph* quotes him as saying "[t]he TV Rebus won't be my Rebus. I don't want voices suddenly thrust upon me" (23 October 1999, p. 71). Rankin later relented, and claims, with reservations, to have enjoyed the production. Critical opinion, however, was divided, and in a succinct article for *Sherlock Holmes* magazine, Mike Ripley calls the production to account:

Black and Blue was not bad—goodness knows there are worse things on television at the moment in the crime field—it's just that I could not forget the book and the book is so much better, so, at the end of the evening, I was disappointed. (p. 13)

The problem was not John Hannah's youth, appearance or performance, but rather the attempt to fit a quart into a pint pot. The scriptwriter, Stuart Hepburn, condensed a 400 page novel into a two hour screen play. Inevitably, the result was over-simplification, with genre clichés replacing the subtleties of Rankin's novel.

Obviously changes would be necessary to make the complex plot manageable within the allotted time. Hepburn's screenplay abandoned Glasgow and Shetland altogether, streamlining the novel into a two-center TV show. Uncle Joe Toal became an Edinburgh heroin dealer, and Ancram's pivotal role as Rebus's potential nemesis was rewritten for Gill Templer. The painful historical realities of the Bible John case were replaced by the wholly fictional character of "The Preacher", who fifteen years previously had terrorized Edinburgh women. As the adaptation opens, Rebus, working out of Craigmillar police station (which seems curiously to have been relocated to Leith), is involved in the hunt for "The Disciple", a copycat killer who has murdered two women—one in Edinburgh and one in Aberdeen. At this point Lenny Spaven is still alive—but not for long. The production has scarcely mapped out the serial killer crisis before Rebus is called to the prison where Spaven is conducting a rooftop protest of his innocence. Having demanded Rebus's presence on his roof, Spaven throws himself to his death with the words "I damn you to hell Rebus". Fortunately Lawson Geddes is more accessible, having been relocated from Spain to the suburb of Fairmilehead, and can consequently protest his beliefs directly rather than through Rebus's memories of the time. The additional complexity of Eamonn Breen's documentary is abandoned, as is the character of Brian Holmes. The marginal character of Angie Riddell, on the other hand, is brought centre stage and made a motivating factor in Rebus's actions. The visit to the oil platform is cut, and there is no space for the analysis of corporate greed and power implicit in the book's account of Major Weir and his daughter. These are substantial changes, but they still left the adaptation with three significant plot strands (the Preacher/Disciple case, the drugs at Burkes Club and Lenny Spaven) and a considerable amount of ground to cover in a short space of time.

As often happens with the miraculous medium of television, everyone — from Rebus to Eve to Uncle Joe Toal — emerged looking a good ten to twenty years younger than the text had suggested. But, while appearances were to some extent glossed-over, in other respects the adaptation revealed a satisfying eye for detail. John Hannah's Rebus was effectively world weary and rumpled. His clothes, his hair and the contents of his fridge all suggested a man too wrapped up in the lives of others to care much about the maintenance of himself. When Rebus arrived to investigate Alan Mitchison's death, the dead man's fridge looked remarkably similar to that of the detective, giving additional resonance to the WPC's scornful comment, "sad bastard". The moment hinted at some fellow feeling between Rebus and the victim, but the pace of the production allowed for no further development. Mike Ripley focuses his criticism on the production's determination to hold on to so much of the plot: "What someone as skilled as Ian Rankin can cogently weave into 400 pages simply cannot be compressed into one and three quarter hours of television" (*Sherlock Holmes* 37, p. 13), and indeed character development was soon hopelessly lost in the race to include a vast catalogue of events. Lawson Geddes provides a typical example. After a leisurely introductory scene in which the actor, David Lyon, exhibited comfortable complacency and a motherly concern for Rebus's welfare, he was not seen again until almost the end of the dramatization. In a rapid and unheralded decline, he sweated out a confession over Rebus's kitchen table, before setting out to commit suicide in his Volvo. It was all over in three minutes.

The production suffered from trying to do too much, but it was not without merit. The locations were particularly effective, avoiding the tourist's-eye view of Edinburgh and capturing some of the bleakness so crucial to the novel. The sense of urban despair present in the text was also carried over into John Hannah's voice-over, the means chosen to try and give some sense of Rebus's interiority to the viewer. The production opened with a rainstorm more appropriate to Glasgow than Edinburgh, and Hannah's downbeat voice:

Shift change at Fort Apache, the Eastern Front, the sort of station you end up in if you don't keep your pockets open and your mouth shut, and in the kind of Edinburgh night that makes Cowdenbeath seem an attractive holiday destination.

The voice-over is a potentially useful technique in terms of giving greater insight into the detective's depressive personality, but here it was more often used as a short-hand method of plot and character development. All we needed to know about Lawson Geddes, Angie Riddell and Joe Toal was encapsulated in a series of wry witticisms that effectively economized on the screen time an actor might need to suggest any personality whatsoever. Ultimately Rebus's mental state was more effectively suggested through visual methods. In a nightmare sequence during his visit to Aberdeen, Rebus is visited by his ghosts and tormentors reciting mantras of blame at the captive detective, who is strapped to a chair as Alan Mitchison had been.

Television and text are not easy to compare — they are fundamentally different media. However, given Rankin's particular concern with the issue of closure, it is worth examining the conclusions of the two narratives, and considering the extent to which they challenge the expectations of reader and spectator respectively. The evidence is ambiguous. In some respects the TV adaptation was more daring than the novel, and it is certainly the case that the TV Rebus was more clearly compromised by his association with the Preacher than Rankin's Rebus had been by his encounter with Bible John. In the screenplay, Rebus meets the Preacher and offers him the address of the Disciple in exchange for a definitive answer to the question of who killed Elsie Rhind. The Preacher confesses not only to the killing of Rhind but also to the framing of Lenny Spaven, and Rebus lets him go in the knowledge that he will kill his unwanted Disciple. Rebus does inform his superiors of what he has learnt, but it takes him some time to do this — time spent standing in the last place he had met his friend, Angie Riddell. This, combined with the final scene's focus on Angie's necklace — sent to Rebus by the Preacher who had reclaimed it from the Disciple — suggests that Rebus's actions were undertaken in revenge for Angie's death.

Yet at the same time that Rebus is implicated in the murder of the Disciple, the adaptation steps back from the moral ambiguity of the killer's escape. The replacement of the actual historical figure of Bible John with the fictional Preacher gives the film-makers scope to impose certainty on Rankin's evasive ending. While the novel left the reader with the suspicion of Geddes's guilt and the absence of closure surrounding Bible John, the screenplay wipes clean the sins of the past. Geddes is driven to suicide by the knowledge he has wronged an innocent man, Rebus's fantastical theories about the return of the father are believed, and the Preacher is halted at the airport by a customs official. His capture is clearly imminent.

Our final views of Rebus also provide a contrast. The novel ends with his attempt to shake off his obsession. After a walk with Gill he returns to the disturbing news of Brian's resignation, after which he settles into his chair and stares out of the window — only to have his reverie broken by an anonymous phone call. The implied caller is Bible John and Rebus is shocked into an attempt to break the "bond" that has been formed by their shared obsession with Johnny Bible:

He heard the other receiver being dropped into its cradle, then the hum of the open line. He stood for a moment, then replaced the receiver and walked into the kitchen, pulled open the cupboard and lifted out the newspapers and cuttings. Dumped the whole lot of them into the bin. Grabbed his jacket and took that walk. (p. 494)

The screen version, by contrast, leaves Rebus firmly in the grip of his shared obsession — even if he has betrayed the Preacher to Gill Templer. Night replaces day, the camera lingers on Hannah's tearful face as he fingers Angie Riddell's necklace, and the final cut shifts to an external shot of Rebus's tenement flat, with the grieving detective alone in his chair at the window.

The shift in emphasis that leaves the TV Rebus locked into the past, while his fictional counterpart reaches a point of relative calm does not only emerge from the contrasts in the final sequence. Rather it has been brought about by fundamental changes in the composition and character of the narrative. *Black and Blue* is a book about the complex relations between men. The TV adaptation turned it instead into a stereotypical celebration of hard-boiled heterosexuality. Angie Riddell, in the novel an early victim of Johnny Bible and an acquaintance of Rebus, became for television the "tart with a heart", and Rebus's only confidante. All the points of human contact that ground Rebus within the novel were removed from the screenplay. Gill Templer replaces CI Ancram as Rebus's internal inquisitor, and their past history is no longer one of friendship. Rather, Gill is rewritten as someone who turned Rebus down for promotion on account of his "attitude problem". Even more disturbingly, the key male characters of Brian Holmes and Jack Morton were uncomfortably conflated into a single cowardly Judas figure, who serves only to reinforce Rebus's status as the legendary loner hero. The television Morton becomes Templer's sidekick and the man who beat up Mental Minto. He never becomes Rebus's friend, and his negative depiction is reinforced in an early scene when the sainted Angie Riddell refers to him as "the filth". The impact of these changes is significant. In Rankin's novel, the monumental masculinity of the hard man is crumbling and under pressure. In Hannah's film its vulnerabilities are safely contained within the boundaries of heterosexual revenge and stoic suffering—both undertaken for Angie Riddell, who in dying has mutated from whore to heroine in the classic manner of hard-boiled narrative.

Although readers of *Black and Blue* were generally disappointed in the adaptation, the critical reception was warm enough to warrant further developments. *The Hanging Garden, Dead Souls* and *Mortal Causes* have all been filmed, and in Rankin's opinion, the productions "seem to be getting better as they go along". But Rankin is not wholly dismissive of the adaptation of *Black and Blue*, and was attracted by some of the developments contained within the script:

In some ways I thought the TV version was stronger than the book, because it had to tighten everything up. But to do that they took some lazy shortcuts. Every second scene seemed to have a prostitute in it, and I don't remember there being quite so many prostitutes in the book! But the scene at the end where Rebus became complicit because he actually gave the address to Bible John [the Preacher], that was a Pontius Pilate moment, which was something that I would never have considered doing in the book, but once I saw it on TV, I thought, that's an interesting angle. It makes Rebus a much darker character.

Rankin is philosophical about the changes made to his novel, concluding that "TV's just a totally different beast". Nonetheless, it is interesting to speculate about the future of Rebus's TV manifestation. In what strikes me as a completely misplaced analogy, *The Sunday Telegraph* once described Rebus as "the Morse of the north" (23 October 1999). Colin Dexter's Inspector Morse novels were turned into best-sellers by their adaptation for television. Rankin, by contrast, was already a best-seller before *Rebus* was broadcast, and the complexity of his characterization and plotting far outweighs that of Dexter's original Morse stories. Perhaps the analogy would be better pursued in the terms of the screen adaptation. Will John Hannah become the "John Thaw of the north" by succeeding in taking a fictional character and turning him into a viable and popular television hero?

5

Further Reading and Discussion Questions

Closure is bullshit

—JAMES ELLROY, 2001

The obvious starting point for any list of further reading must be Rankin's other Inspector Rebus novels. Although each novel stands comfortably alone, there are benefits to be gained from a sequential reading, and a full list in order of publication can be found in the bibliography. The first novel, *Knots and Crosses* (1987), provides key background information about Rebus's family and his experiences in the SAS. In contrast to *Black and Blue*'s focus on fathers and sons, this is a novel about brothers, but it is noticeable that although already haunted by his past, Rebus's masculine boundaries are far more firmly in place. The second novel, *Hide and Seek* (1991), explores the Jekyll and Hyde character of Edinburgh and introduces Rankin's ongoing concern with conspiracy and power. Probably the most impressive of the novels that preceded *Black and Blue*, however, are *Mortal Causes* (1994) and *Let It Bleed* (1995). In *Mortal Causes*, Rebus's army career returns to haunt him in an investigation that exposes Edinburgh's sectarian divide, while in *Let It Bleed* we see Rebus at his most anti-authoritarian, battering away at a conspiracy that embraces the great and good of the city.

Also of interest are Rankin's other novels, in particular the Jack Harvey books, which have now been reissued by Orion. These are exciting and well-written thrillers, and although they lack the psychological complexity that Rebus has developed over the years, they have much to recommend them — not least of which is the pleasure of spotting characters later re-used by Rankin in other contexts. *Blood Hunt* (1995), for example, even invents a parallel life for Gordon Reeve, the hapless 'villain' of *Knots and Crosses*.

Readers interested in the background to *Black and Blue* should pursue the list of references provided by Rankin at the end of the novel (p. 498). Of these, Andrew O'Hagan's *The Missing* (1995) is particularly interesting for the insight it provides into the mythology of Bible John. Little is known of the killer, but O'Hagan is not concerned with speculating about identity. Rather he examines the impact of the unsolved murders on the community, seeing the killings as a loss of innocence for the Glasgow of the 1960s:

A community living with an uncaught serial killer is a place where many feel under threat, and many under suspicion. Long after the murders seem to have stopped, killers stay on in the minds of those who lived, and feared a brutal end to life, under their dark spell. This happens with all killers, but much more so with ones who are never caught: they can always kill again. Their power remains, never revealed, never dispelled. . . . The murderer, having no known identity, takes little parts from the identities of everyone. (p. 54)

Alternative perspectives on the recent history of Scotland and Scottish identity can be found in the work of Tom Nairn, and Craig Beveridge and Ronnie Turnbull, while an introduction to the state of the nation at the time of *Black and Blue*'s composition is provided by David McCrone's *Understanding Scotland: The Sociology of a Stateless Nation* (Routledge, 1992). As the title suggests, McCrone's book has been overtaken by recent events, but it remains an excellent account of Scotland and its culture in the 1990s. Useful essays on Scotland can also be found in Susan Bassnett's *Studying British Cultures* (Routledge, 1997). These books, however, pre-date devolution, and the restoration of the Scottish Parliament in 1999 has brought fundamental change to Scotland's identity and agendas. Now that the nation has far greater autonomy and is no longer situated in clear-cut opposition to Westminster, accounts of contemporary Scotland are having to be rewritten as debates and agendas that preoccupied the nation for nearly three centuries are replaced with new political and cultural concerns.

From this point onwards constructing a list of further reading becomes more complex, as Rankin's writing straddles such diverse traditions. Readers interested in the development of the hard-boiled detective novel should undoubtedly begin with Raymond Chandler and Dashiell Hammett. The best of Chandler is, arguably, represented by *The Big Sleep* (1939) and *Farewell, My Lovely* (1941), while Hammett's *The Maltese Falcon* (1929) provides an ideal antidote to Chandler's somewhat romanticized vision of the tough-guy. It is also worth reading Chandler's self-justifying but wonderfully entertaining article, "The Simple Art of Murder" (1950), republished in the short story collection, *Pearls Are A Nuisance*. This is the article that gave to posterity such immortal phrases as "down these mean streets a man must go who is not himself mean, who is neither tarnished nor afraid", and although Chandler has a few blind-spots as far as his detective is concerned, he is very funny on the subject of the classical murder mystery. For an alternative perspective, couched in equally polemical prose, readers should consult George Orwell. His essay, "Raffles and Miss Blandish" (1944), published in *The Decline of the English Murder and Other Essays*, provides a valuable counter-blast challenging the celebration of "toughness", and linking the violence of hard-boiled fiction to moral crisis and a totalitarian worship of power.

The post-Second World War influences on Rankin are also predominantly American. Lawrence Block's Matt Scudder novels shed light on the development of Rebus and Big Ger Cafferty, while almost anything by James Ellroy will illustrate the quick-fire prose and brutal realism that so impressed Rankin. Good examples of Ellroy's ability to meld history and fiction are provided by *The Black Dahlia* (1987) and *American Tabloid* (1995). The first of these is a powerfully violent re-imagining of a gruesome murder from the late 1940s, while the second takes the gloss off the Kennedy years, rewriting one of America's most romantically mythologized eras from a criminal perspective. Ellroy is a disturbing writer for a number of reasons, not least of which is his ability to create a sense of self-disgust in his readers. The books are often as funny as they are horrific — and the pleasure gained in reading them sits uncomfortably next to an awareness of the boundaries he has transgressed in his depiction of criminal acts and attitudes.

Ellroy in turn was deeply influenced by Thomas Harris's *Red Dragon* (1981), a novel he described in 1997 as "the greatest suspense novel ever written", and which he credits for giving new dimensions to the psychopathology of serial killers in fiction. Harris's novel is an excellent starting point for anyone interested in the concept of the serial killer, but good examples of this sub-genre can also be found in Britain. Val McDermid's *The Mermaids Singing* (1995), which won the Gold Dagger in 1995, and her sequel *The Wire in the Blood* (1997), are particularly recommended. McDermid constructs a multi-focalized narrative, providing diverse perspectives on the police enquiry alongside sharp and effective delineations of character. The books are violent and disturbing, but

they shock the reader into unexpected sympathies and a new awareness of the meanings of power. Equally impressive is McDermid's
1999 novel *A Place of Execution*, which threads past and present
together in a new investigation of a long-closed case, raising questions about justice, punishment and the rights of the victim.

McDermid, like Rankin, originally hailed from Fife, but these
two writers are merely the tip of an impressive iceberg of Scottish
writing sometimes dubbed "tartan noir". Manda Scott's first novel
Hen's Teeth (The Women's Press, 1996) was short listed for the
1997 Orange Prize for fiction, while Denise Mina's *Garnethill*
(Bantam, 1998) won the CWA John Creasey Memorial Dagger for
the best first crime novel. Both of these novels are set in Glasgow,
but an earlier recipient of the John Creasey award, Paul Johnson,
provides a highly innovative slant on Edinburgh policing in his
series of novels set in the new world order of the 2020s. The first of
these, *Body Politic* (1997), describes a fragmented Britain, broken
up into warring city states. Edinburgh, now governed on the prin-
ciples of the Enlightenment and underpinned by the teachings of
Plato, is dedicated to the servicing of its tourist industry. Locals live
in Orwellian conditions, while anything goes for the visitors and,
not surprisingly, Johnson's investigator, Quintillian Dalrymple, has
a somewhat ambivalent attitude to the city. Dalrymple fits neatly
into a long line of disaffected detectives, and Johnson's carefully
created futurescape marries humour and horror in its delineation of
a not-so-brave new world.

The status of godfather amongst Scottish literary detectives, however, is usually reserved for William McIlvanney's Jack Laidlaw.
Built firmly on the tradition of the Glasgow hard man, Laidlaw is
also an autodidact much given to philosophy and introspection. He
features in three novels, *Laidlaw* (1977), *The Papers of Tony Veitch*
(1983) and *Strange Loyalties* (1991), all of which are deeply concerned with issues of moral responsibility and the breakdown of

community. McIlvanney has an impressive ability to evoke the city, and his Glasgow landscapes make a pleasant change from the blood-spattered granite of Edinburgh, even if his detective becomes aggravatingly self-righteous and his female characters remain obstinately rooted in the stereotypes of self-sacrificing mother, warm-hearted whore, and emasculating shrew.

Amongst the writers of contemporary Scottish fiction, two others deserve particular mention. One is Christopher Brookmyre, whose angry satirical novels could easily be shelved under crime fiction. *Quite Ugly One Morning* (1996) is a thoroughly entertaining read, and like much of Rankin's fiction it exposes the hypocrisy and double standards of respectable Edinburgh society. The other writer, of course, is Irvine Welsh, whose *Trainspotting* (1993) was an acknowledged influence on Rankin. More recently Welsh has produced his own "police" novel, *Filth* (1998), which bears almost no resemblance to any model of the crime genre. Rather it is an impressive but overlong delineation of the breakdown of a truly monstrous manifestation of the Scottish male. Welsh juggles the real and the surreal, describing the mental and physical collapse of his protagonist in gruesome detail. Ian Rankin remembers reading reviews that claimed the novel was a "deconstruction of Rebus", a statement which he finds incredible, and indeed, it is hard to see any viable grounds on which to sustain such a claim.

Although Rankin himself is yet to be subject to any sustained critical attention, there is a growing body of literature on crime fiction that offers useful routes into an analysis of his novels. John G. Cawelti's groundbreaking study *Adventure, Mystery and Romance: Formula Stories as Art and Popular Culture* (University of Chicago Press, 1976), remains the best introduction to genre form, and is particularly relevant to *Black and Blue* as it includes chapters on the western as well as the crime novel. Also recommended as introductions to both hard-boiled and golden age fiction are Stephen Knight's excellent *Form and Ideology in Crime Fiction* (Macmillan, 1980), Julian Symons *Bloody Murder: From the Detective Story to the Crime Novel* (Pan Books, 1992) and Martin Priestman's admirably succinct survey *Crime Fiction: From Poe to the present* (Northcote House, 1998). T. J. Binyon's *'Murder Will Out': The Detective in History* (Oxford University Press, 1989) does exactly what the title suggests, providing an encyclopaedic and highly readable account of the detective's progress from amateur to professional. The book is necessarily superficial, but a fascinating resource for the curious. Peter Messent's collection of essays, *Criminal Proceedings: The Contemporary American Crime Novel* (Pluto, 1997) throws light on some of the writers who have influenced Rankin, while gender issues in the crime novel are considered at length in my *Twentieth-Century Crime Fiction: Gender, Sexuality and the Body* (Edinburgh University Press, 2001) — which also contains a chapter on serial killing.

For an introduction to masculinity and popular culture see Anthony Easthope's entertaining and succinct *What A Man's Gotta Do* (Routledge, 1990). Also useful on this subject are Harry Brod and Michael Kaufman's fascinating collection of essays, *Theorizing Masculinities*, (Sage, 1994); R. W. Connell's substantial survey *Masculinities* (Polity, 1995) and Lynne Segal's *Slow Motion: Changing Masculinities, Changing Men* (Virago, 1990).

Last, but not least, anyone approaching Rankin's fiction should acquaint themselves with Robert Louis Stevenson's *The Strange Case of Dr Jekyll and Mr Hyde*. It, along with James Hogg's *The Private Memoirs and Confessions of a Justified Sinner*, is by far the most pervasive of Rankin's literary influences. The lessons of Jekyll and Hyde permeate *Black and Blue*, along with almost every other Rebus novel, and it is instructive to consider the different ways in which Stevenson's narrative colors each of Rankin's novels.

INTERVIEWS, WEBSITES AND GUIDED TOURS

Fans of Rankin's work will find some useful information on his website, *www.ianrankin.com*. The website connects to short reviews and a number of interviews with the author. One of the best of these, an American interview by J. Kingston Pierce entitled "Ian Rankin: The Accidental Crime Writer" can be reached directly on *www.januarymagazine.com/profiles/ianrankin.html*.   Rankin   talks about his early years in Cardenden and mentions some of the other influences on his career, including Ernest Tidyman's *Shaft* (1970) and the literary criticism of Umberto Eco. Rankin also discusses some of his other work, including his excellent, and sadly out of print, novel *Watchman* (1988) and his radio plays for the BBC. *www.twbooks.co.uk/authors/irankin.html* is a useful repository of Rankin links — including further reviews of his novels and an entertaining piece by the author on the filming of *The Hanging Garden*. Crime discussion lists are many and various, but amongst the biggest and best is *DorothyL*, which offers wide-ranging debates and reviews amongst writers and aficionados.

On paper, a substantial interview with Rankin, conducted in the aftermath of the success of *Black and Blue* and *The Hanging Garden*, can be found in *Scotlands* 5.2 (1998), and he also features in Issue 7 of the magazine *Crime Time*. Recent newspaper and magazine profiles include *The Sunday Telegraph Magazine*, 23 October 1999, *The Bookseller* 9 February 2001, *Scotland on Sunday*, 25 March 2001 and *The Guardian*, 21 April 2001.

And, finally, the guided tour! Mercat Tours of Edinburgh are now running a range of Rebus Tours. Visitors to Edinburgh can book three different walking expeditions of two hours duration that will help them to "uncover another side to Edinburgh than that shown in the tourist guidebooks". The sights on offer include St

Leonard's Police Station, the City Mortuary, Edinburgh University, Warriston Cemetery, the Water of Leith, the docks and, of course, the Oxford Bar—where refreshment is *not* included. The walks pause for readings from Rankin's novels and one of the tours appropriately includes a visit to the boyhood home of Robert Louis Stevenson. To conceive of fiction as a tourist attraction requires quite an imaginative shift—but the detective novel has always depended upon a powerful sense of location, and part of Rankin's success can certainly be attributed to his ability to evoke a complex, visceral and unconventional Edinburgh. The tours are a tribute to Rankin's reinscription of the city, and they form a bizarre but substantial statement of the impact achieved by his work.

DISCUSSION QUESTIONS

- In a recent interview Rankin said that he wanted to "take in not only the whole of Scotland, but Scottish politics and industry and all sorts". How successful is Rankin in depicting the diversity of modern Scotland? Can *Black and Blue* be described as a "state of the nation" novel? And if so, what is the state of the nation?

- In his review of *Black and Blue*, Liam McIlvanney described Rankin's treatment of the Bible John case as "superficial and unsatisfactory". How do you respond to this criticism?

- *Black and Blue* is predominantly "focalized" through the perspective of Rebus. The most notable exceptions to this are the Bible John sections. How do you respond to this voice? Is it disturbing, and if so, why?

- A very different outside perspective is provided by Lawson Geddes's letter (pp. 453–57). How reliable a narrator is Geddes? Is it possible to establish the "truth" of the Spaven case? To what extent is the reader manipulated by Geddes's appeal to the memory of the victim?

- I discussed some aspects of the friendship between Rebus and Morton, but there is also evidence in the text to suggest that Rebus attempts to manipulate Jack and the situation in which he finds himself. What are we to make of comments such as: "Jack wouldn't shop him. The man had lost too much self-respect already" (p. 293)?

- Would you describe Rebus as a selfish or egotistical character?

- How effective is the novel's soundtrack? Rankin uses Rebus's record collection as an emotional shorthand, a way of succinctly evoking the mood of the detective or the state of his surroundings. Do you think the technique works, and if so, what does the music tell us about Rebus?

- Rankin likes to play games, to pun and make connections within his texts. In this light, what might we make of the epigraphs he uses, and section headings such as "The Whispering Rain", "Dead Crude" and "The Panic of Dreams". What, for that matter, should we make of the novel's title? Why call the book '*Black and Blue*?

- In his review of *Black and Blue* Peter Whitebrook described Rebus as "a morally complex man, a Calvinist, driven by a conviction, augmented by experience, that retribution is not only more just but more effective than rehabilitation". Would you agree with this assessment? Is it appropriate to describe Rebus as a Calvinist, and if so, why?

- Compare Rebus to other contemporary detectives, for example William McIlvanney's Jack Laidlaw or Sara Paretsky's V I Warshawski. What do the similarities and differences between them tell us about the direction of contemporary crime fiction and Rankin's desire to push the boundaries of the genre?

- How appropriate do you find the term "Edinburgh gothic" as a description of Rankin's work?

- Robert Louis Stevenson's *Dr Jekyll and Mr Hyde* has been widely cited as one of Rankin's key influences. How important is the theme of duality in *Black and Blue*? What other influences and themes can you detect?

- Discuss the role of violence in *Black and Blue*. Is it gratuitous or does it serve a purpose in terms of plot, character or theme? What can be achieved through the depiction of violence? And to what extent is violence depicted as an integral part of masculine identity?

- Allan Massie thinks Rankin would be well advised to kill off Cafferty. Do you agree?

- *Black and Blue* is not the end of the Rebus story and the detective continues to evolve. What do you see as the future of Rebus and Rankin's Edinburgh novels?

Bibliography

Works by Ian Rankin

All references within the text are to the Orion paperback editions of Rankin's novels.

Novels:

The Flood. Edinburgh: Polygon, 1986.

Knots and Crosses. London: The Bodley Head, 1987; New York: St Martin's Paperbacks, 1995.

Watchman. London: The Bodley Head, 1988.

Westwind. London: Barrie and Jenkins, 1990.

Hide and Seek. London: Barrie and Jenkins, 1991; New York: St Martin's Paperbacks, 1997.

Wolfman. London: Century, 1992. Reissued as *Tooth and Nail*, London: Orion, 1998; New York: St Martin's Dead Letter Mysteries, 1996.

Strip Jack. London: Orion, 1992; New York: St Martin's Paperbacks, 1998.

The Black Book. London: Orion, 1993; New York: St Martin's Paperbacks, 2000.

Mortal Causes. London: Orion, 1994; New York: St Martin's Paperbacks, 1997.

Let It Bleed. London: Orion, 1995; New York: St Martin's Paperbacks, 1998.

Black and Blue. London: Orion, 1997; New York: St Martin's Paperbacks, 1997.

The Hanging Garden. London: Orion, 1998; New York: St Martin's Paperbacks, 1999.

Death Is Not the End: An Inspector Rebus Novella. London: Orion, 1998; New York, Minotaur Books, 2000.

Dead Souls. London: Orion, 1999; New York: St Martin's Minotaur Series, 2000.

Set In Darkness. London: Orion, 2000; New York: Minotaur Books, 2000.

The Falls. London: Orion, 2001; New York: Minotaur Books, 2001.

Short Stories:

A Good Hanging and Other Stories. London: Century, 1992.
Herbert in Motion and Other Stories. London: Revolver, 1997.

Writing as Jack Harvey

Witch Hunt. London: Headline, 1993.
Bleeding Hearts. London: Headline, 1994.
Blood Hunt. London: Headline, 1995.

Select Criticism

Brod, Harry and Michael Kaufman (eds). *Theorizing Masculinities*. London: Sage, 1994.

Cawelti, John G. *Adventure, Mystery and Romance: Formula Stories as Art and Literature*. Chicago: University of Chicago Press, 1976.

Chandler, Raymond. "The Simple Art of Murder". In *Pearls are a Nuisance*. Harmondsworth: Penguin, 1964: 181–99.

Connell, R. W. *Masculinities*. Cambridge: Polity Press, 1995.

Easthope, Anthony. *What A Man's Gotta Do*. New York and London: Routledge, 1992.

Knight, Steven. *Form and Ideology in Crime Fiction*. London: Macmillan, 1980.

Light, Alison. *Forever England: Femininity, Literature and Conservatism Between the Wars*. London: Routledge, 1991.

Messent, Peter. *Criminal Procedings: The Contemporary American Crime Novel*. London and Chicago: Pluto, 1997.

O'Hagan, Andrew. *The Missing*. London: Picador, 1995.

Orwell, George. "Raffles and Miss Blandish". In *The Decline of the English Murder and Other Essays*. Harmondsworth: Penguin, 1965: 63–79.

Plain, Gill. "An Interview with Ian Rankin". In *Scotlands* 5.2 (1998): 106–21.

Plain, Gill. *Twentieth-Century Crime Fiction: Gender, Sexuality and the Body*. Edinburgh: Edinburgh University Press, 2001.

Ripley, Mike. "Telly 'Tecs . . . investigating detectives on the small screen". In *Sherlock Holmes* Issue 37, 2000: 12–13.

Silverman, Kaja. *Male Subjectivity at the Margins*. New York and London: Routledge, 1992.

Willett, Ralph. *The Naked City: Urban Crime Fiction in the USA*. Manchester and New York: Manchester University Press, 1996.

Whyte, Christopher. "Masculinities in Contemporary Scottish Fiction". In *Forum For Modern Language Studies*. XXXIV: 1998 (34:3): 274–85.